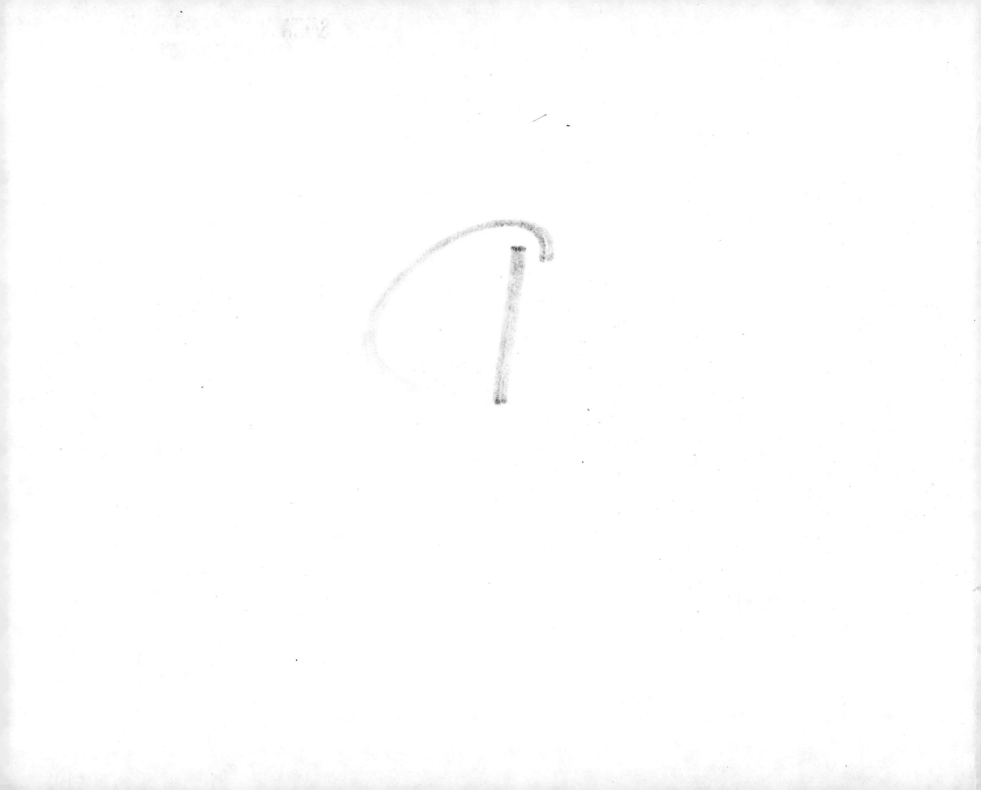

KIDTOPIA

KIDTOPIA

'Round the Country and Back
Through Time in 60 Projects

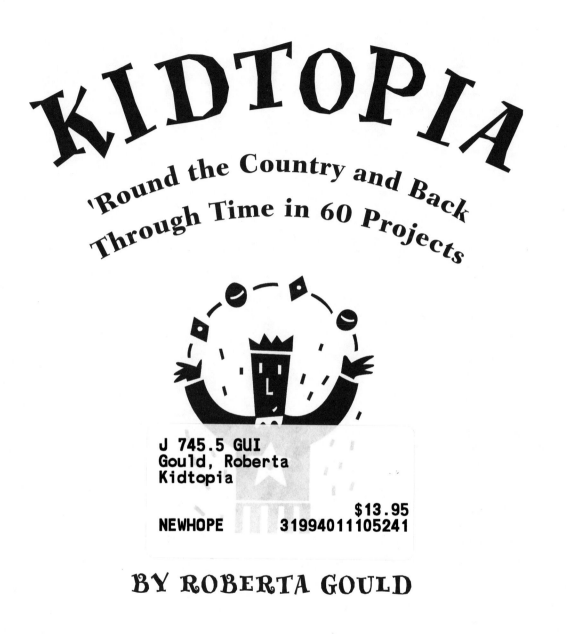

BY ROBERTA GOULD

 TRICYCLE PRESS
BERKELEY ★ TORONTO

Tricycle Press
P.O. Box 7123
Berkeley, CA 94707
www.tenspeed.com

Book design by Catherine Jacobes
Cover photography by Karen Preuss
Typeset in Brody, Buffalo Gal, Circus Mouse, Fairfield, Farmhouse,
La Bamba, Retablo, Rosewood, Syntax, Whimsy, Wonton
Clip Art: Image Club, Hoopla Fringe, and Hoopla Cuts

Printed in Canada

Library of Congress Cataloging-in-Publication Data

Gould, Roberta, 1946-
    Kidtopia: 'round the country and back through time in 60 projects / by Roberta Gould.
        p. cm.
    Includes bibliographical references and index.
    Contents: Tea taxes and eye patches: Colonial America -- Eat, drink, and be merry: North Country pioneer life -- Hain't much, but you're welcome to it: Southern country roots -- Tenderfeet and greenhorns: The California gold rush -- Lizards and skulls: The American Southwest -- Living on the edge: The Pacific Rim.
    ISBN 1-58246-026-4 (alk. paper)
    1. Handicraft--United States--Juvenile literature. 2. United States--History--Juvenile literature. [1. Handicraft. 2. United States--History.] I. Title.

TT23.G68 2000
745.5—dc21
00-044719

THANKS TO:

Family and friends: David, Ben, Nathaniel, Peter, Mom, Debbie, John, Elly, Julie, Naomi, Chick, and Mani.

Editors: Nicole, Cybele, Kate, and Zippie

The children at Lake School: Adriana Michelle Avila, Amy J. Mejia, Ana R. Ruano, Antoine L. Robinson, Breaunna Michelle Austin, Brenda Muñoz, Brittany Terry, Chang Saechao, Cheng Lai Saechao, Corey Spears, DaMonica Mason, Daryl Shaun Myers Jr., David Hackett, Derrick L. Vassey, Evonté L. Brown, Ferrari May Suiex Pharn, Fou Linh Saechao, Frances Perez, Gina Saechao, Ieisha Kelly, Jarroue Holloway, Javontae Felix, Jeffery Hartwell, Jenny Nungaray, Jessica Areas, Jesus Javier Ayala, Joanne Dolor, John Casey Jones, Jorge A. Trujillo, Keri Saechao, Leon Traysean Small, Luke Tyler Hissom, Marshala A. R. Williams, Marvin Escalante, Mary Ernie L. Navarro, Morgan B. Wilson, Moung Tong Saechao, Mykel Chamber/Barrett, Raul De Leon, Raymundo Jimenez, Roslind A. Woodard, San On Saechao, Sapna Kumari Sharma, Shanidra Q. Brown, Shaquille Omar Page-Wilson, Simone Woods, Stephanie L. Hernandez, Stephanie Yien Fou Liew, Tanzania Avington, Teresa Montes, Tomisha Pickett, Tristan Chao, Wynona Marie Bucay, Zoe Steverson.

Bobbie's Amusing Muses: Acacia Quien, Aisha Khan, Alana Trieschmann, Alice Reichman, Allison Menzimer, Amaya Blanco Ramirez, Amber Marion Bacon, Amy Rinaldi, Annie Chin, Annie Pennell, Anya Black, Anya Goldstein, Ari Usher, Arwen Thoman, Asa Kalama, Audrey Beil, B. B. Said, Ben Kalama, Ben Rudiak-Gould, Benjamin Derish-Luby, Bethany Lynn Woolman, Bianca Smith, Bill Holden-Stern, Brigette Stump-Vernon, Caitlin, Carl Gould, Carmen Ruda, Carlos I. Sempere, Caroline Thow, Carolyn Audrey Thompson, Carolyn Earnest, Carrie Meldgin, Carrie Peterson, Casey Jackson, Charlie Buck-Bauer, Clare Nicole Kruger, Colleen Smallfield, Cor Despota, Daniel Lawrence, Daniel Reichman, Darleen Ashlee Aragon, Daveed Daniele Diggs, David Meldgin, E. A. Grinstead, Eileen Beil, Eli Liebman, Elizabeth, Elizabeth Brokken, Elizabeth Prindle, Ellen Streit, Emily McKeown, Emily Walters, Emily Zubritsky, Emma Silvers, Fiona Gladstone, Francesca Danby, Genevieve Michel, Hannah K. Moore, Hester Chambers Mills, Honey Bee Evans, Iain Burke, Ilana Caplan, Isa Guardalabene, Jacob Delbridge, Jacob Winik, Jacquelyn Rohrer, Jed Loveday-Brown, Joe Holden-Stern, Jonathan Ball, Joy Proctor, Kaitlin Friedman, Karen Nakasato, Kari Gjerde, Karl Robinson, Karolyn Wyneken, Katherine Winkelstein-Duveneck, Katie Jensen, Kimberly Mei Aller, Kiri Jones, Kory Sutherland, Krista Smith, Kyle Kemp, Lauren Finzer, Leif Pipersky, Lucia Graves, Lyal Michel, Lydia Arce, Marcus Toriumi, Marjorie Rose Gomez, Marta Blanchard, Matthew Delbridge, Max Green, Maya Dobjensky, Maya Sanchez-Haller, Meir Berman, Michael Clement, Michelle Kim, Michi, Mika Endo, Mira Bullen, Mitchell Green, Miya Frank, Miya Kitahara, Molly Anixt, Molly Gould, Molly Munch Di Grazia, Nariman Safizadeh, Natalie Buck-Bauer, Nathan Rynerson, Nathaniel Rudiak-Gould, Nicholas Danby, Nicole Berger, Osiris Henderson, Parker Menzimer, Paula Robinson, Peter Rudiak-Gould, Rachel Krow-Boniske, Rachel Schultz, Rachel Shoshana Berman, Rebecca Krow-Boniske, Richard Michel, Robin Anne Fink, Romana Ferretti, Ryan Mueller, Sam Blau, Sandy, Sara Schultz, Sarah Adams, Sarah Dobjensky, Sarah Leff, Sarah Rose Barrett, Sarah Streit, Sean Smith, Sherry Lee Aragon, Sierra Liebman, Sierra Miley-Boland, Solange LeRoux, Solomon Wong, Sophia Perkis, Sophie Linder, Sophie Weiss, Sophie Winik, Spencer McNamara, Stefan Goldberg, Summer Jackson, Tara Mongkolpuet, Tess, Tessa Jordan Breedlove, Vanessa Wellbery, Vivienne S. Carlsen, Walker Shapiro, Waylon James Bacon, Yoshi Smith, Zach Walters, Zoe Balance, Zoe Griffith, and anonymous.

CONTENTS

INTRODUCTION

Kidtopia means kids' place. A place where kids have fun: hiding pirates' treasure, telling scary stories, scooping gold off the ground, making glittery sugar skulls, becoming a famous movie star.

This book is a time machine that will take you back to times and places you have never been. You'll travel around the United States and back into American history. You can be a child in colonial times making candles for the dark winter approaching. You can be a pioneer gathering wild fruit and making your own pie. You can live in the Southwest and weave your homespun yarn into your own blanket.

When you look back at people who lived long ago, you may wonder how they knew how to do all the things that they did. How did they gather and prepare their food? Did people actually make

doughnuts, instead of buying them at the store? How did they make clothes? This book will prove that you can make almost anything yourself.

While you learn old traditions, you will make things in your own special way. Your candles may have artistic lumps and bumps. Your pie may have a silly design on the crust. Your movie can be wild and crazy.

In today's world many things are done for us, so we lose our sense of self-sufficiency. People used to rely more on themselves, and you can too. The projects in this book teach many old skills that put you more in charge of your life. It feels wonderful to make things for yourself. Once you have made some of the projects in this book, you will realize how talented you are!

NAVIGATING THROUGH THIS BOOK

Choose your difficulty level:

★ **Level 1: Elementary, My Dear.** If you are at least seven years old, these projects should be easy.

★★ **Level 2: Talent Search.** If you are about nine years old (or just plain talented), these projects should be easy. If you are younger, you may want a little help from grown-ups or an older friend or sibling.

★★★ **Level 3: Ego Booster.** These projects are just a little bit harder (and you'll sometimes wish you had four hands or a magic wand), but you get to feel really proud when you finish!

This book is full of interesting tidbits and tips. Watch for these:

- **A Long Time Ago:** The ways things were in olden times.

- **Once upon a Time:** Suggestions for good books to read about the past.

- **Fun Fact:** Facts that are just plain fun.

- **Did You Know?** Snippets of science for the curious.

- **Save the Earth:** Ecologically sound ideas that will help the planet.

- **Party Idea:** Ways to use projects for parties.

- **Caution:** Important warnings about potential dangers. If you are careful and use the tools in the right way, you will be just fine.

- **Yeah!** An even easier way to make the project.

- **Oops!** Little mistakes to avoid.

2

YOUR TOOLS

The Most Useful Tool Award goes to the low-temperature glue gun. It is really wonderful, but it can be a little dangerous.

- Be sure to use the low-temperature kind of glue gun. Even so, the tip end of the glue gun and the melted glue are very hot, so don't touch them. If you do so accidentally, run cool water over the burn immediately.

- Have a grown-up help you set up the glue gun where you can use it safely. You need to be careful that the electrical cord is not in the way when you are cutting with scissors. A really neat way to get the cord out of the way is to use a metal cord holder for an iron. It's a contraption that holds the cord up in the air while you are ironing. You can buy one from your local hardware store.

- Make sure that you unplug the glue gun when you are done.

Here are some other useful tools:

- Serrated "steak" knives work like saws for cutting through hard materials and aren't as dangerously sharp as straight-bladed cutting knives. Their pointed ends are good for piercing cardboard and plastic.

- Permanent pens have wonderful bright colors, and they write on many unusual surfaces. They are rather smelly, and it's probably not a healthy smell, so open the windows or work outside.

NOT TRASH, TREASURE

Keep your eyes open! Many things that usually get thrown away can be used to make wonderful art. When you look at things closely, you discover many uses for them. Even an empty dental floss container can be made into a doll backpack, tiny portable phone, or small robot. Before you throw anything away, look at it. Is it intriguing, cute, small, interesting? Put it in your art room. All through this book you will see surprising uses for "junk." Here are some things to save for projects.

Food Packaging

PLASTICS

- gallon milk jugs
- berry containers with attached lids
- medium-size tubs with lids
- yogurt containers
- tops from squirt bottles
- Styrofoam food trays

METAL

- cookie tins
- aluminum foil bits from packaging
- tin cans
- take-out food container handles
- "throwaway" aluminum pie pans from purchased pies
- small candy boxes or cocoa tins

MISCELLANEOUS

- wax coating on cheese, washed
- plastic and metal lids from cartons, bottles, and jugs
- small- or medium-size glass bottles with lids
- round containers (made out of cardboard, plastic, or metal) with plastic lids, from oatmeal, coffee, and hot chocolate
- aluminum foil, candy wrappings, plastic netting, shaped macaroni, bread clasps, sections of drinking straws, toothpick pieces, bottle caps

Party Leftovers

Lots of cool materials are used at parties and thrown away. Help with the cleanup, and get the goodies. Just remember to wash the stuff!

- old candles
- shiny and other pretty wrapping paper
- plastic or glass bottles (8- to 12-ounce) with screw tops that don't leak
- glass bottles from juice, sparkling cider, root beer, and maple syrup
- corks from wine and champagne
- plastic cups
- wires from burned-out sparklers
- small partly burned birthday candles, burned wooden matches, glitter, confetti, and bells

Ragbag Finds

- worn sheets
- socks that have lost mates
- pillows or quilt stuffing
- buttons
- old Velcro
- worn backpacks
- old jeans
- old suspenders, cloth belts, and ties

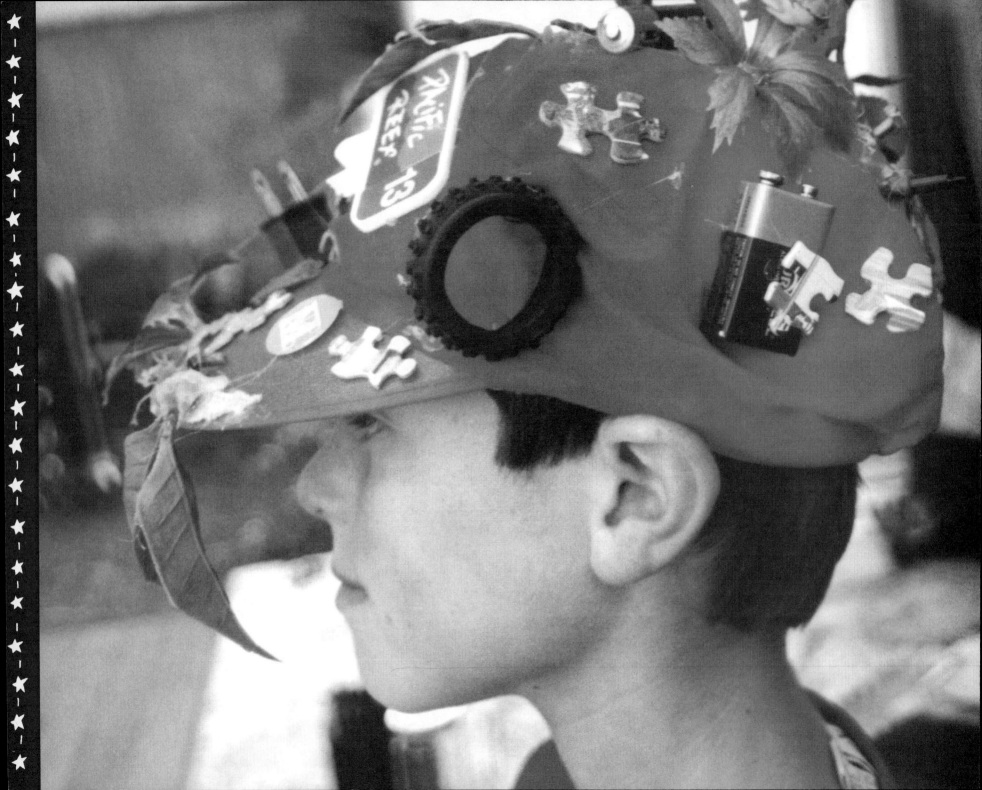

Ragbag Finds, continued

- wire coat hangers
- old pieces of cloth
- old long-sleeved shirts
- worn-out pairs of your shoes
- old Halloween costumes
- old men's shirts, fancy dresses, huge pants, black skirts, and black jackets
- old glasses, dark glasses, belts, canes, purses, gloves, neckties, scarves, jewelry, hats, tails, beautiful shoes, crazy shoes, and pillows
- shoulder pads removed from clothing
- worn-out knitted sweaters
- velvety cloth, ribbons, buttons, sequins, yarn, rickrack, lace, scraps of cloth, leather (real or fake), fur, cloth flowers, zipper pulls, and snaps

Household Haul

- baby wipe boxes
- cardboard tubes
- cardboard boxes and flat packaging pieces
- small empty and clean bottles from shampoo samples, extracts, and medicines
- burned-out incandescent lightbulbs

- old wooden blocks
- worn-out bicycle tires
- old tennis balls
- heart-shaped candy boxes, shoebox lids, frame-shaped Styrofoam, and clear plastic boxes
- unwanted cassette tapes
- dental floss containers
- small plastic pieces, Styrofoam curlicues, small tiles, old stamps, metal clasps from manila folders, old decks of cards, keys, magazines, sock hooks, small screws and nails, bobby pins, marbles, paper clips, aquarium gravel, stamps, stickers, and puzzle pieces

Carpenter Castoffs

- window screens, washed
- scrap wood
- white or tan pull-down window shades

Garage Sale Goodies

Go to garage sales and charity bazaars at the end of the day, when folks want to just get rid of stuff. (Go earlier to buy *good* stuff!) Try to find some of these:

- old necklaces
- old car seat covers made of hundreds of wooden beads

Things to Ask For

Prepare a list of things you want, and don't be too shy to ask for them from parents, friends, neighbors, and friendly merchants.

- plastic "comb" book bindings at photocopy stores
- boxes at cigar stores
- old inner tubes at auto tire repair shops
- wood scraps in the free box at carpentry shops and lumberyards
- scraps at foam mattress stores
- burned-out bulbs at lighting and lamp stores
- old tires at bicycle repair shops
- after Valentine's Day, heart-shaped boxes from people you know

- multicolored wire, in bundles of one hundred wires, from the telephone company
- after winter holidays, gift-wrapping paper and blown Christmas bulbs from people you know

Other Cool and Crazy Stuff

- things from nature, such as twigs, shells, shiny rocks, crystals, pressed flowers, flower petals, small fern leaves, tiny feathers, cones, dried corn, dried beans
- little pieces taken apart from broken toys and electronic equipment

Join Forces

Find out if your neighborhood has an artists' and teachers' recycling headquarters, where people bring things that they can't use and would otherwise throw away. They give the headquarters their "junk" for free and pay a small amount to take home a bag of art goodies. You may have a center like this in your community, because they are a really good way to protect our environment.

A Smart Art Room

Once you have managed to collect wonderful stuff, you're ready to get organized. Sorting things helps to make them more available for use. Ask a grown-up to help you set up shelves and sort your stuff.

Have a corner or room or shack or nook where creativity is easy because everything is there. The ideal art space has

- a big table in the middle covered with an old sheet, cloth, or shower curtain so no mess is permanent.

- lots of shelves bursting with goodies in labeled shoeboxes and milk jugs. Cut the narrow opening of the milk jug to make more room to reach in, but leave the handle in place because it's handy. Some foods, such as popcorn, vegetable oil, and juice, come in see-through gallon jugs that are very nice for storing attractive materials.

- an organizing cabinet with drawers for tiny treasures. You can buy one at a hardware store or home improvement center.

- a messy floor that no one looks at or comments about. A messy floor is the sign of a creative mind!

The ideal spot for your art room is central enough to be handy for constant use, *and* separate enough so you don't have to stare at the mess or need to clean it before guests arrive. It is also wonderful if your creative space has easy access to the outside so you can spill outdoors whenever possible.

1

TEA TAXES AND EYE PATCHES: COLONIAL AMERICA

....

WHEN EUROPEANS CAME TO AMERICA, they settled along the coast and found a beautiful but harsh country. With the help of Native Americans and using their own ingenuity, they made a good life in their new home. The Atlantic Ocean was an important part of their lives. They used the sea both for their food and for trade with other countries. Some captains took their families on their ships because they were going to be gone for so long. Their quarters were actually pretty nice, but life at sea could be hard for the families. To make the trip fun, the children were allowed to bring their favorite pets. The coast was busy with sailing ships, and our favorite bad guys, pirates, flourished.

CRAFTiNG APRON

★ ★

🕐 5 minutes

Have you ever been in the middle of making something wonderful and had to stop to search all over for scissors or some other tool? You know how frustrating that is. The first project in this book is a Crafting Apron. You'll use a small carpenter's apron to hold scissors, tape, pens, glue sticks, and other tools that you'll want handy for making the other projects in this book. Then you can always put your hands on the tool you need when you're in the middle of exciting creativity.

What You'll Need

- a small canvas work apron. Inexpensive carpenter's aprons can be bought in hardware stores. The small sizes have plenty of space for your tools and are about the right size for kids.

- yarn: two pieces, each about 18 inches long

- tools to put on your apron that will be useful for the projects in this book:

- two pairs of scissors (see "Wise Tool Use"). Buy good strong scissors, and treat them well so they last a long time.

- adhesive tape

- marking pens

- glue stick

- (optional) pliers

- (optional) a small screwdriver

- (optional) a small hammer. A small size will work just fine and probably be a little safer for you.

- (optional) a low-temperature glue gun, for making loops smaller

Caution: Get grown-up help. The glue comes out hot, and the tip of the gun is hot.

- (optional) permanent pens or cloth paints, for decorating the apron

What to Do

1. Use the yarn to tether each pair of scissors to a side loop of the apron. Tie one end of the yarn to a side loop, and one end to the scissors handle. Make sure the tether is long enough for you to use the scissors while you're wearing the apron. Side loops are usually used for holding a hammer, but most work well to hold scissors.

Oops! If your loops are too large and the scissors fall through, you can glue or sew across each loop to make it shorter.

2. If you wish, decorate your apron using permanent pens or cloth paints.

3. Arrange the other tools for projects and activities in the pockets.

4. Put on your apron, and start making things!

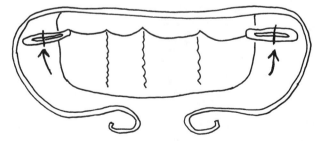

Wise Tool Use

It's best to have two pairs of strong scissors on your Crafting Apron. Label one **Cloth** and the other **Wire.** You need two pairs because cutting wire makes scissors dull, and then it is hard to cut cloth with them. So use the **Wire** scissors to cut wire and all sorts of other tough materials, such as thin wood, plastic, and aluminum pie pans, and use the **Cloth** scissors for cloth and paper. This way you will have tools in good shape for your needs.

Popcorn Trick

★

🕐 15 minutes

Popcorn is amazing stuff. When the Spanish explorers came to America, they were given popcorn necklaces as presents. You can string popcorn, using a needle and thread, to make a necklace or to decorate a holiday tree. Or wow your friends with this simple trick.

What You'll Need

- 1 full-to-the-top cup of milk
- 1 cup of plain popped corn

What to Do

Just drop the popcorn into the milk one piece at a time. The cup will not overflow! Now try adding another cup of popped corn. Can you fit it in without making the milk overflow?

A Long Time Ago...

Native Americans grew corn, beans, and pumpkins (or squash) together in a group, because these plants help each other grow better. The beans take nitrogen out of the air and put it into the soil where the corn and squash can use it. The corn makes a natural trellis for the beans to grow onto and up, so they get more of the sunlight they need. The squash mulches the ground, keeping it moist, which helps the corn and beans. They are three best friends, each different, each helping the others.

When Native Americans ate grains from wild grasses, they would parch them by tossing them in a basket with hot rocks until the grains popped. This was one of their favorite foods.

Fun Fact

The milk does not really take up all the space in the cup! Just as you can stir lots of sugar into a cup of milk and it will dissolve and disappear into the spaces in the milk, so the starch in the popcorn dissolves.

New (Olde) Ways to Get Around

★

🕐 **As long (or as a short) as you want**

Since the invention of the car, people have fallen out of the habit of using their own power to go places. Walking and riding a bike (or horse) are very satisfying ways to get around. Have you tried walking or biking to places that you usually go to by car? The weird thing is that the places sometimes seem closer! And places that are a hassle to get to by car may be a fresh, smooth, invigorating, and interesting bike ride away.

What You'll Need

- plastic bottles with secure lids to carry water and juice

- some yummy food

- a small backpack

- weather gear, such as a hat, sunscreen, sunglasses, a raincoat

- (optional) an adventure book to read while you rest

- a bike

- a helmet

- a really fun grown-up

A Long Time Ago...

In early colonial times, people had some interesting ways of getting around. One idea, called **Walk and Ride,** used only one horse for two people. One person would walk and one would ride the horse. When the person riding the horse got ahead after a while, he or she would tie the horse to a tree in an obvious place and start walking. The horse would get a rest until the first walker arrived and climbed on to ride. She or he would pass the friend and ride ahead for a while. The two alternated until they reached their destination. You might want to try this with four people and two bicycles so that you will have company the whole time. (Caution: Check with a grown-up first to plan a safe journey.)

Once upon a Time

The Hobbit by J. R. R. Tolkien: This is absolutely one of the best adventure books! After you read it you can go on to read the amazing trilogy that follows: **The Lord of the Rings.**

The Exploits of Moominpappa by Tove Jansson: This is also one of a series, so there are lots more to read, if you like it. It has a quirky sense of humor.

What to Do

- If you have enough time, you can get almost anywhere on foot or bicycle. You just start and you don't worry about how long it takes. On the way you might find ripe berries, sparkly rocks, velvety leaves, trees full of fruit, small parks with drinking fountains and slides. You might run from a barking dog, make the acquaintance of several cats, or watch birds.

- You can have a goal: the lake at the county park a few miles away, your favorite blackberry patch, or the top of the hill. Rest when you're tired and go when you're ready.

- Or you can just wander this way and that, exploring, deciding at each corner which route looks fun. Make a zigzag path through your town, turning right at the first corner, left at the next. You'll be surprised at what you discover as you explore where you are and then see what's around the next bend.

- Try walking in the rain. A tame city becomes a much wilder place in the rain. Instead of thinking you need to come *in* because it's raining, try going *out*. Discover streams gushing over and around leaves in the gutter, producing water wheels and big puddles. Find jewels of water drops on tree leaves and flowers. Let yourself get wet.

Ground Rules for Grown-ups

Kids are sometimes nervous about going somewhere "far away" by foot or bike. They may think they can't make it. Try to give them the sense that there is no hurry and that there are lots of interesting things to see and do along the way. If the process is enjoyable, they stop worrying about getting there. When they do arrive, they feel triumphant!

When you hike by yourself or with other adults, you may like to set a pace and not stop often. Kids like a totally different style. They like to run to the big rock and climb all over it, look around, be silly together, and then charge down the hill to the stream, where they jump from bank to bank, look at the tiny fish, and notice the spider hanging over the water. Give it a try too—you might enjoy this kid-centered way of hiking.

When school classes take field trips, they often depend on having parents drive the children, even if the concert or museum is only a few miles away. Is there a way for the kids to walk or bike there? It's fun, and best of all, the children are too tired to squirm during the concert!

Dipped Candles

★★

🕐 1 hour

In previous centuries, an important fall activity was making candles for the coming winter. You've probably burned candles and eaten meat and never thought there was a connection. But when people raised their own animals, they would butcher them in the fall (after the first freezes, so that the cold winter temperatures would preserve the meat). They boiled the fat from the meat until the water evaporated and the gunk sank to the bottom. This purified fat (called "tallow") was used to make candles. That once was a big job for each household; now you can do it for fun!

What You'll Need

- paraffin. Buy some in the canning section at the grocery store, or recycle wax from old candles or from the coating on some cheeses (wash it first). Beeswax is a nice addition. Maybe you can get some from a local beekeeper.

- crayons (to give color to the wax)

- wicks. Buy them at a craft store or use package-wrapping string.

- tall tin cans

- a grown-up

- a double boiler or a large pan that a metal cooling rack will fit into

- a stove or hot plate (see Caution)

- water

- stirring sticks (use old chopsticks)

- (optional) a food-warming tray

- an outdoor place to work, or lots of newspaper to cover the table and floor. Wax is messy!

Caution: For this project you must have a grown-up to help. You will be using boiling water, which can burn your skin. Warm wax is soft and moldable and fun to work with, but you have to be careful. The main danger comes from letting the wax get too hot. *Never* heat wax in a can or pot directly on the stove and never heat it in the microwave. You must heat it in a water bath. This guarantees that the wax can't get hotter than boiling water. Water boils at 212°F (100°C); above that temperature it becomes steam. But wax heated directly on the stove could get hotter and eventually explode and catch on fire!

What's in a Candle?

Eulachon, or "candlefish": These slender silvery fish were prized by natives of the northwest coast because of their high fat content. The streams where the fish flourished were owned by certain groups, who went there when the fish were running in the spring, to get their year's supply. They used the fish oil mostly for eating but also for light and heat.

Tallow: American colonial households saved all the uneaten fat from turkey, goose, passenger pigeon, deer, bear, fish, sheep, pig, and cattle for candle making. In the fall they boiled all the rancid pieces of fat down to make tallow. They used the tallow for candles or for fuel in oil lamps. Unfortunately it smelled really awful during the rendering and while burning. It also attracted mice, who would eat the candles. Tallow candles had to be kept in a mouseproof box.

Bayberry: The tiny berries of the wax myrtle plant soon became a favorite candle material for the early American colonists because the wax smelled good when it was burned. It took thousands of bayberries to make one candle. Kids did a lot of the harvesting work. The colonists loved the smell of bayberry candles so much that they made laws about the berry patches. In some areas, anyone who picked the berries before they were ripe was charged a fine!

Whale: Inuit people living in the Arctic used whale oil for heat and light. New England whalers brought back a white, waxy substance (called spermaceti) from the head of a whale that the colonists used to make candles. These candles would "give out more light than three tallow candles, and have four times as big a flame" (**Home Life in Colonial Days** by Alice Morse Earle, p. 42).

Beeswax: Wax made by insects has been used for candles for 5,000 years and is still one of the favorite candle material.

Waxy paraffin: This is one of the many things made from petroleum, which is formed underground by tiny water organisms changing over millions of years into a rich fuel. In the 1800s, Americans used another petroleum product, kerosene (similar to today's jet fuel), to illuminate the evening, and it is still used for camping stoves and heaters.

Kukui nut, or "candlenut": Found in Hawaii, these nuts are so full of oil that you can just skewer one on a bamboo splinter and light it!

Olive oil: In Europe and the Middle East, Jewish people used olive oil in lamps and for their Chanukah celebrations.

What to Do

1. Break the paraffin into pieces that fit into your tin cans. To break it easily, freeze the paraffin first. Then drop the pieces on the sidewalk and they will break.

2. Fill the cans 3/4 full of wax.

3. With grown-up help, place the cans in a double boiler with water in both the bottom and the top pans, or in a large saucepan with a small metal cooling rack and at least 2 inches of water in it. Warm the pan over low or medium heat just until the wax is melted. Do not overheat! Make sure the water does not boil dry (see Caution)!

4. Choose crayons to color your candle wax. It takes several crayons to color each can of wax. Use one color per can or more shades to get exciting new colors. Peel the crayons, and add them to the wax. Let them melt, and stir the color in.

5. Place the cans on a food-warming tray, if you have one, or ask a grown-up to bring the pot of hot water with the cans of melted wax to where you're working. Use caution around the hot water.

6. Dip a piece of wick into the melted wax, and pull it out. Hold it up and let it cool in the air for about 1 minute.

7. Dip the wick in the wax and out again, letting the wax cool for a minute after each dip. Dip quickly. If you leave the wick in too long, the hot wax will melt the previous layers and the candle will get thinner!

8. Repeat until the candle is as thick as you want it to be.

9. Hang the candle by the wick until it's completely cooled; otherwise it may slump or bend.

Circle Around

Here's a fun way for a group to make candles. You all walk around the table in a circle, dipping in the hot wax in turn and letting the candle cool till you get back to the wax.

19

Tin Can Lantern

★

🕐 **1 hour**

Make a lantern with holes that let out sparkly bits of light. The lantern also keeps your candle from being blown out by gusts of wind.

What You'll Need

- smooth-sided cans with the tops removed—for example, cans from mandarin oranges (11 ounces), sweetened condensed milk or coconut milk (14 ounces), or whole clams (28 ounces)

- (optional) shredded newspaper

- wire. Handles from take-out food containers work perfectly, or get flexible but strong wire from a hardware store.

- candle stubs. Short fat ones work best.

- a black permanent marker

- water

- nails—several sizes to make holes of different sizes

- a hammer (see Caution)

- pliers

- cloth rags

Caution: Hammers can hurt! For this project you will be tapping the nails fairly softly, because you don't want to dent the can or make the nail go very far in.

What to Do

1. Plan your pattern, and mark it on the can with the permanent marker. A design with a lot of holes is very pretty. Traditional lanterns had very complex patterns.

2. Fill the can with water to 1/2 inch from the top. Freeze it for 1 to 2 days until it is really solid.

Smashing New Method: Instead of freezing your can with water, you can fill it with shredded newspaper, pour in some water, and then pound the gooey mess down with a hammer (see Caution) until it's really tight. Repeat until the can is stuffed. This way you don't have to wait for water to freeze, so you can start your lantern right away.

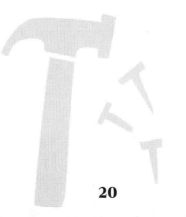

3. When the ice is thoroughly frozen (or the newspaper filling is thoroughly packed), hammer holes in the can following the pattern you made. Hammer gently so that you don't dent the can. Wrap a rag partway around the can to keep it from rolling. Nail quickly if the can is full of ice, before the ice melts. Hammer the nail in only about 1/8 inch, and take it back out.

4. Hammer two holes near the top of the can on opposite sides for the handle.

5. Let the ice melt away (about 15 minutes), or pull out the newspaper pulp.

6. Use pliers to shape the wire into a handle shape, and attach it.

7. Put a candle in the lantern. Secure it by dripping some wax or putting a small lump of clay in the bottom. Light it, and take it to a dark place so you can enjoy the magic sparkling of the light coming through the holes.

A Long Time Ago...

Early Americans got their tinware from traveling peddlers. Everyone looked forward to the tin peddler's visits, because he would tell wonderful stories and bring them the latest news from near and far.

Back in the old days, people bartered rather than using money. Whenever they had extra of something they produced, they could trade it for other things they needed. They could even get new tinware for their old rags! It is hard to believe now, but rags were very valuable in colonial times, because they were used for making paper. There was never a large enough supply for the papermaker's needs. (Read more about papermaking in the chapter "Living on the Edge.")

SAILORS AND PIRATES

Everyone seems to be fascinated by life on board the old sailing ships. It was a hard life, but full of adventure. We especially look back romantically at the life of the pirates. Learn some of the skills and arts of the sailor, and enjoy the fun parts of being a pirate. You won't have to worry about being marooned on an island or having to learn to walk on a peg leg!

OCEAN IN A BOTTLE

★

🕐 **30 minutes**

If you don't have an ocean handy, you can make your own Ocean in a Bottle. In fact, it's a lot easier to fit an ocean in a bottle than to fit a ship in a bottle. This simple project is a lot of fun. I think you'll be surprised at how interesting it is to watch the wave action in your bottle. And when you look through a magnifying glass, you may believe that you see creatures swimming around!

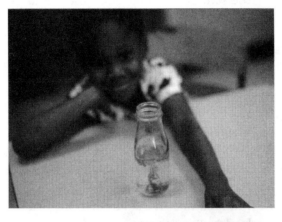

Once upon a Time

If you like adventure stories, read **Kidnapped** by Robert Louis Stevenson. Most of the adventure involves an escape through Scotland, but at the beginning our hero gets kidnapped on a sailing ship. Luckily for him, it capsizes and frees him from being forced to work (perhaps for years) aboard the ship. The practice of kidnapping sailors from waterfront saloons was fairly common, because not enough people wanted to crew on ships—the work paid too little and was hard and dangerous!

Did You Know?

Some tiny organisms in the ocean emit light when jostled. If you are lucky, you'll be in the right place at the right time to see this beautiful magical happening. You can see it anywhere from Cape Cod (on the Atlantic Ocean) to Seattle (on the Pacific Ocean) to Hawaii. You might notice it as you watch waves splash. It is surprisingly bright. Recently my son and I saw it when our friend's dog swam in the phosphorescent (glowing) sea. The dog seemed to be wearing a marvelous bright coat of stars!

What You'll Need

- a plastic or glass bottle (8- to 12-ounce) with a screw top that won't leak

- water

- blue food coloring

- oil (the cheapest kind of cooking oil)

- sand

- things that looks like miniature beach flotsam and jetsam: twigs, shells, toothpick pieces, small plastic pieces, and bits of Styrofoam

- anything that makes you wonder whether it will sink or float, such as small pieces of chalk and rubber band bits

- (optional) glitter

- (optional) a magnifying glass

What to Do

1. Fill the bottle 2/3 full of room-temperature water.

2. Drop in the food coloring, *slowly*, drop by drop. Watch the color float through the water and disperse in pretty patterns.

Oops! It is so much fun watching food coloring mix into water that you may keep adding drops until the water is almost black. If you dilute the food coloring with water before you start, this won't happen as quickly. If the water does become darker than you want, add more water and pour out the excess.

3. Slowly add the oil to the water, leaving 1–2 inches of air space. It's fun to watch the oil bubble down and then come back up to the top.

4. Add the sand, and watch it fall to the bottom. Then add the flotsam and jetsam and odd bits to see what floats and what sinks.

5. You can add glitter to make a very interesting ocean.

6. Screw on the lid tightly, and make waves in your ocean. Shake it more to get storms!

7. Use the magnifying glass to look at your ocean.

Fun Fact

After sailors had been at sea for a while, they ran out of fresh food and ate mostly salted meat. If this went on too long, they would get a disease called scurvy. It was caused by a lack of vitamin C, but they didn't know that. They did know that fresh food made them better. Eventually they started taking lemons on trips, but before that, they got the needed vitamin C from—guess what—raw onions and potatoes. "The onions were genuine and fresh…we…ate them raw…. And a glorious treat they were…. We were perfectly ravenous after them. It was like a scent of blood to a hound. We ate them at every meal, by the dozen…." (from **Two Years before the Mast** by Richard Henry Dana, the true story of a nineteen-year-old who sailed from Boston to California in the 1830s).

Fun Fact

Flotsam is any part of a wrecked ship or cargo found floating on the sea. **Jetsam** is anything that has been thrown overboard on purpose (probably to lighten the load during a storm). There is actually a law that says you can keep either one if you find some, so help yourself!

Pirate Treasure Chest

Imagine that you are a pirate, hiding treasures that no one else will be able to find, even if they search for hundreds of years! The first thing you need is a pirate chest.

★

🕐 30 minutes

What You'll Need

- a small container with an attached lid. Try cookie tins, baby wipe boxes, cigar boxes, or the plastic fruit containers that cherries and blueberries sometimes come in.

As many items for decoration as you can find:

- bits of aluminum foil. You can recycle these from packages.
- some velvety cloth and ribbons
- stickers
- gold-, silver-, or wood-colored contact paper
- glitter and beads

- fabric paint or acrylic paint and old clothes or a paint smock to wear while using them
- a low-temperature glue gun (with adult supervision only!), white glue, or double-sided sticky tape

Caution: Get grown-up help. The glue comes out hot, and the tip of the gun is hot.

What to Do

- Decorate the treasure box, inside and out. If you have a low-temperature glue gun, it's very easy to attach everything to a plastic or metal box. The inside can be lined with velvety cloth. The outside can be decorated with beads, foil curlicues, glitter, and anything else that you like. Check out the ones in the photos to see ideas that other kids have come up with. Every treasure box will be different and wonderful. Glue stuff on until you like how it looks.

- If you don't have a glue gun, use regular glue or double-sided sticky tape to hold things on. And decorate with stickers, contact paper, and fabric paint.

Make the Treasure

★

🕐 **30 minutes**

Now that you have your Treasure Chest, you can fill it to the brim with treasure galore.

What You'll Need

A collection of "valuables," such as

- old necklaces and costume jewelry

- pennies

- plastic and metal lids. Save them from cartons, bottles, and jugs.

- gold foil. Save the wrappings from candies and chocolate money.

- silver (aluminum) foil from gum wrappings

- shiny wrapping paper

- curtain rings, leftover plastic spools from adhesive tape, and other round plastic or metal rings

- cardboard

- shiny rocks and crystals

- (optional) a low-temperature glue gun

Caution: Get grown-up help. The glue comes out hot, and the tip of the gun is hot.

What to Do

1. Make treasure coins by covering the pennies and lids with gold and silver foil.

2. Make rings by covering curtain rings, tape spools, and other ring-shaped things with gold or silver foil. Crinkle up candy wrappings in bright reds, greens, and blues to make jewels for the rings.

3. Make a dagger out of cardboard covered with silvery paper, and encrust the hilt with dazzling wrapping paper jewels.

4. Heap your Treasure Chest full of necklaces, jewels, coins, rings, daggers, shiny rocks, and crystals. Fill it with all the glittery stuff you can find!

Hide the Treasure~ Make a Treasure Map

★★

⏱ 1 hour

Pirates hid their gold so that they would not have to give it up if they were caught. But sometimes they couldn't return to retrieve the booty. Even today, some people go looking for famous pirate hoards. It doesn't happen often, but every once in a while they find treasure! In this activity you'll hide your treasure and draw a tricky map.

What You'll Need

- a large, sturdy piece of paper. Home-made paper is good (see page 121).

- a pen or pencil

- matches and a candle

- a friend with a spray bottle of water

- a grown-up

- dirt and cold coffee

- (optional) pinking shears

- (optional) an iron

What to Do

1. Find a place to hide your treasure in your backyard or neighborhood.

2. Make a diabolically difficult map. Try some of these ideas:

   - Show your neighborhood as it would have looked before the houses were built. Show the streams, large trees, hills, but *not* the houses and streets. Or put on the map only a few of the things in your neighborhood, such as the pets found at each house, but not the houses, so that only a very observant person could figure out where things are.

Once upon a Time

If you want to read about treasure hunting, chapter 25 in **The Adventures of Tom Sawyer** by Mark Twain has an especially wonderful description of the feeling you get when you're hunting for treasure. Other great books are **Treasure Island** by Robert Louis Stevenson, **The Gold Bug** by Edgar Allan Poe, and **Alfred Hitchcock and the Three Investigators in the Mystery of the Dead Man's Riddle** by William Arden.

- Rub dirt into the paper. Maybe tear part of the map. Pour coffee on the map to darken it.

- Light the candle, have a friend stand by with a spray bottle full of water, and round up a grown-up to help while you burn the edges of your map. If you cut the edges with pinking shears first, it will be easier to control where the map burns. Flames go up, so hold your paper so that it will burn toward an edge away from your fingers, a little at a time, not toward the center. You might also want to obscure part of the map with a burn to add challenge to reading it. Your friend should spray the flame out if the map starts burning too much. A candle works much better than a match, because it won't burn out too quickly and will give you more control.

- If you want to make a map that needs to be folded to reveal the secret, start with a very large piece of paper. Make a tuck across the middle and draw the map on the folded paper, then unfold it, and iron it flat. You can fill in the blank parts of the paper with misleading information. See the illustration.

- Make part of the map in code. You can make up a code or get a book on codes.

3. Invite your friends and neighbors for a party with a treasure hunt.

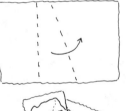

Codes

Here are a few of the many wonderful and confusing codes in Martin Gardner's **Codes, Ciphers and Secret Writing:**

- Mirror Writing: "Go left" would be written   GO LEFT = TFEL OG

- One Up Substitution: This is a simple but confusing code. Just substitute b for a, c for b, etc. So if you want to write "Behind the large rock," you write "Cfijoe uif mbshf spdl."

- Names: Each word of the real message is preceded by a proper name. Other words are added to make the message confusing. "Go north 10 feet" could be written "Which way will Joe go in the car with Sue, north? We could pay Amy 10 cents to find some clean socks for Jake's feet.

- Tic-Tac-Toe: "Climb tree" would be written

A	B	C
D	E	F
G	H	I

J	K	L
M	N	O
P	Q	R

S	T	U
V	W	X
Y	Z	?

CLIMB TREE =   L L·Γ ⅃U   ⊔·Γ□□

- Rot 13: Shift the alphabet by thirteen to encode it. Use the same method to decode it (because there are twenty-six letters in the alphabet).

A = N

B = O

C = P

D = Q

etc.

DIG DOWN FIVE FEET

QVT QBJA SVIR SRRG

2

EAT, DRINK, AND BE MERRY: NORTH COUNTRY PIONEER LIFE

THE NORTH COUNTRY, which includes Upstate New York, Michigan, Wisconsin, and Minnesota, has long and cold winters. Pioneer life there was hard but also a lot of fun. If you read *Farmer Boy* by Laura Ingalls Wilder, you will probably start to feel very hungry, because Almanzo and his family get to eat a ton of really delicious-sounding food. They had a busy and productive life that made each person proud of his or her accomplishments and very, very hungry!

MILKING

Barnyard animals were an important part of the self-sufficient lifestyle of North Country pioneers. The animals did work plowing and hauling and provided food and materials for clothing. They were also the family's source of milk. Even if you live in the city, your home may not be as far as you think from a live cow or goat. Contact the 4-H club closest to you for the names of friendly owners. Find your local branch in the phone book under Four-H, or on the web at 4h-usa.org. Ask if they'll let you learn to milk one of their stock. Most owners and animals will be patient as you learn to milk.

MILKING PRACTICE WITHOUT A COW

★

🕐 15 minutes

Before tackling an actual barnyard animal, you can practice the technique of milking.

What You'll Need

- a rubber or vinyl glove
- a pin
- water
- a rubber band

What to Do

1. Prick a hole in each finger of the glove (but not the thumb). These are the four teats of your "cow." (Goats have only two teats.)

2. Fill the glove with water, and tie the top closed with the rubber band.

3. Squeeze the top of one "teat" closed with your thumb and forefinger, then squeeze closed your second, third and fourth fingers in that order. The water will come spraying out. It feels a lot like actually milking a cow or goat! You can practice milking with both hands if someone holds the glove (and moos?).

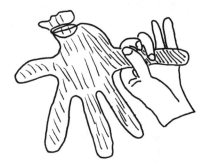

MILKING A LIVE COW OR GOAT

★ ★ ★

🕐 30 minutes

What to Do

1. To milk the animal, you must close the teat at the top and squeeze the milk out. Do not pull down on the teat. It feels wonderful to lean into a warm cow's side and hear the milk go swish, swish into the bucket.

2. Be sure to drink some of that delicious fresh milk! You can strain it through a clean cloth into a glass jar and cool it immediately in the refrigerator.

Fun Fact

How many legs does a stool need? Have you ever noticed that a three-legged stool is more stable than a four-legged one? Most milking stools are three-legged, but one invention was a one-legged milking stool. The legs of the person milking were supposed to provide the other two legs, but it's awkward to do. When I tried it, I promptly fell off backwards into the cow-yard muck!

Party Idea

If the weather is warm, have a water fight using your "cows."

CRANK ICE CREAM

★★

🕐 1–1/2 hours

I scream, you scream, we all scream for ice cream. North Country pioneer kids enjoyed this treat very much. It must have been really delicious, made with their own fresh milk.

What You'll Need

- the ingredients for the ice-cream recipe you prefer (see the next column)

- ice. Freeze lots of ice cubes, or make chunk ice in wax cartons or plastic jugs from milk.

- 2 cups rock salt

- a hand-cranked ice-cream freezer. Some hardware stores and some fancy kitchen stores sell these. Or see if you can borrow one from friends or neighbors.

- (optional) a cardboard box and a hammer to break up the chunk ice

- a pillow, towel, or soft rag

Orange Sherbet

3 cups fresh-squeezed orange juice

1 cup sugar

juice of 2 lemons

1 quart low-fat milk

Vanilla Ice Cream

1/2 gallon whole milk

1 cup sugar

1 tablespoon real vanilla

A Long Time Ago...

Ice cream was first invented in China 4,000 years ago. It was made with milk and gooey rice and was available only to the very rich. Finally, 3,300 years later, the Chinese made fruit ices and sold them to ordinary people on the streets. Marco Polo brought this idea to Italy in the 1400s, and the Italians brought ice cream to the rest of Europe. Ice cream really became popular in America after Thomas Jefferson brought back a recipe from France. (Wow, the Declaration of Independence **and** ice cream!)

What to Do

1. Mix the ice-cream ingredients together, and pour into the canister. Put the lid on tight, so no salt will get into the ice-cream mixture. Place the canister into the cranking bucket.

2. If you made chunk ice, put the containers in the cardboard box, and hit them with the hammer. Breaking up the ice while it is still in the container keeps the bits of ice from flying all over. Eventually the container will break. Then shake the broken ice out into the box.

3. Layer the ice with the rock salt around the outside of the ice-cream canister. Make several layers of ice and salt.

4. Start cranking the freezer. Put the pillow, towel, or rag on the freezer, and have one person sit on it to keep it stationary. Crank the handle at a medium speed for about half an hour. Luckily, the mixture can sit for a few minutes without cranking, if you need a rest.

5. When you can't stand cranking any longer, eat the ice cream. If it's milk-shake consistency, serve in a big cup with a straw.

Did You Know?

Salt makes the ice-and-water mixture colder than the normal 32°F (0°C) for freezing. Without the salt, it would take much longer to cool and freeze the ice cream.

MAKE FRESH DOUGHNUTS

★★

🕐 1 hour

The Dutch in America called doughnuts *olykoeks*. You may not speak Dutch, but I bet you can translate this word! Olykoeks were walnut-size balls, so the English-speaking pioneers called them doughnuts. Everything went along fine until 1847, when a fifteen-year-old kid told his mom that her doughnuts were too soggy in the center and suggested that they would cook better if she made a hole in them. This kid later became a sea captain and lived to the age of eighty-nine, but his claim to fame was the hole in doughnuts.

What You'll Need

This makes about 30 doughnuts.

- 2 eggs
- 1 cup sugar
- 2 tablespoons melted butter
- 5 cups flour
- 3 teaspoons baking powder
- 1/2 teaspoon nutmeg
- 1/2 teaspoon salt
- 1 cup buttermilk (or milk)
- cooking oil (safflower or corn)
- (optional) powdered sugar
- (optional) cinnamon sugar (1 teaspoon cinnamon mixed with 2 tablespoons sugar)
- an eggbeater
- 2 bowls, a large bowl and a medium
- a mixing spoon
- a grown-up
- a deep-fat fryer (or a deep pan and a candy thermometer)
- paper towels

What to Do

1. Beat the eggs in the large bowl. Mix in the sugar and butter. Mix the flour, baking powder, nutmeg, and salt together in the medium bowl, and stir them into the egg mixture. Add the buttermilk, and stir until well mixed. The batter should be stiff but easy to mold. If it is gooey, add more flour; if it is too tough, add more milk.

2. Divide the dough into 30 lumps. Each lump can be formed into whatever shape you want: traditional rings or other nutty shapes. Any shape will work, but it can't be too large or the dough will be raw on the inside. (Remember the story of the hole!)

Caution: A grown-up must be in charge of this step. It is very dangerous!

3. Heat the oil in the deep-fat fryer to 375°F (190°C). Gently lower each doughnut into the oil. If you're having a party, cook one person's doughnuts at a time. In a couple of minutes the doughnuts will rise to the top, indicating that they are almost done. Let them brown a little more, and then lift them out carefully, and drain them on paper towels.

4. If you like, sprinkle the doughnuts with powdered sugar or cinnamon sugar. Eat them while they're still warm!

Party Idea

You can make the dough ahead, invite some (nutty?) friends over, get a grown-up to be in charge of the deep-fat frying, and find out how good fresh, hot doughnuts taste.

GATHER A WILD HARVEST

Pioneers always took advantage of the wild food they could find. Wild strawberries may be small, but each berry has more flavor than a large store-bought one. Wild berries are free, and you can eat as many as you want!

BERRY PICKER'S BUCKET

★

🕐 15 minutes

It's a lot of fun to find wild berries. Ask a grown-up to help you look in vacant lots, on stream banks, next to railroad tracks (but not too close!), and in other wild areas. You have to be an explorer to find places other people haven't found. Often the best spots are not far away, just slightly hidden, so they aren't obvious. If you find a spot where others have picked already, try looking higher up in the bushes (bring a box or ladder) or lower down in the bushes. A lot of berries are hidden under leaves, so if you get down low and look up into the plants, you may discover a handful or bucketful. Berry picking is greatly speeded up if you make a holder that goes around your neck, free-ing both your hands to pick.

What You'll Need

- a medium-size plastic tub with a lid

- a shoelace, string, or thin rope, 2 to 3 feet long

- a hammer and a nail

What to Do

1. Punch two holes in the plastic tub near the rim on opposite sides, using the hammer and nail.

2. Thread the shoelace through the holes and knot it on the inside.

3. Hang your bucket around your neck, and pick a lot of berries.

4. Use the lid to protect the berries during transit home. Make sure you wash your berries before eating them.

39

TALL TREE FRUIT PICKER

★

🕐 15 minutes

The easiest way to pick fruit that grows higher is to use this wonderful tool. Explore in your neighborhood for fruit trees that don't get harvested. Look in a nearby wild area for an abandoned orchard. Don't worry if the fruit is not perfect as long as it tastes good. If the trees are in someone else's yard, ask your parents to help you ask for permission to pick the fruit.

What You'll Need

- a tin can (about 20- to 29-ounce size)
- (optional) shredded newspaper
- 3 short pieces of thin wire, like the wire that is wrapped around store-bought vegetables.
- a tall stick, straight and sturdy (Rough or square-shaped wood works best.)
- a plastic bag or small piece of cloth
- a hammer and a nail

What to Do

1. Using the hammer and nail, make three pairs of holes in the side of the can along the seam, as shown in the illustration. You can stuff the can with wet shredded newspaper to keep it from denting.

2. Thread a short wire in each hole and out the nearby hole. Wrap the ends around one end of the stick, and twist tightly to fasten the stick to the can. You may need grown-up help.

3. Pad the bottom of the can with the plastic bag or piece of cloth to protect delicate fruit.

4. Hold the stick so the piece of fruit is right inside the can, and jiggle it until the fruit falls into the can. If it doesn't come off easily, it's probably not ripe.

A Long Time Ago...

Pioneers used hooked sticks to remove dead branches from their fruit trees. This helps protect the trees from disease. In the old days, in England, a law allowed commoners to gather wood in the king's forests as long as they took only dead wood. It was OK for them to pull down dead branches from the trees, but they had to use a reaper's hook or a shepherd's crook, not a saw. The phrase "by hook or by crook" comes from those long ago days, but now it means "by any means, fair or foul"!

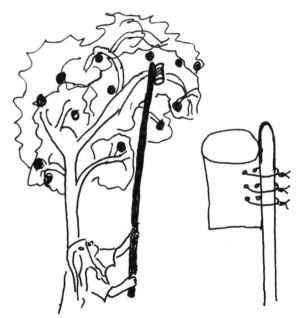

BAKE AN ALL-AMERICAN APPLE PIE

★★

🕐 2 hours

North Country families ate a lot of pies—for breakfast and lunch and dinner. Wow!

CRUST

This recipe is enough to make a bottom crust for a large pie or a top and bottom crust for a medium pie.

What You'll Need

- 1 cup flour
- 2 tablespoons butter
- 2 tablespoons oil
- 1/4 cup cold water (tap water and an ice cube)
- a medium-size bowl
- a spoon
- waxed paper (or plastic wrap)
- a cutting board or clean table
- a rolling pin
- a pie pan. You can reuse a "throw-away" aluminum pan from a purchased pie.

Once upon a Time

Laura Ingalls Wilder wrote many wonderful books about her pioneer childhood in the 1870s. **The Little House in the Big Woods** tells about Laura's young childhood in Wisconsin. **On the Banks of Plum Creek** tells about her school-age years in Minnesota. **Farmer Boy** is the story of the Upstate New York childhood in the 1860s of Almanzo Wilder, her husband-to-be. Look at a map of the United States to see how very far north you would be if you lived in Upstate New York, Wisconsin, or Minnesota.

What to Do

1. Put the flour in the bowl. Add the butter, and mix with your clean fingers until the butter is in tiny pieces.

2. Add the oil, and continue to mix by hand.

3. Add the cold water, and mix with the spoon until the dough all sticks together. If it is too dry, add a little more water, 1 teaspoon at a time.

4. Form the dough into two small balls. If your pie pan is very large, form one ball using all the dough for the bottom crust.

5. Tear two sheets of waxed paper (12 by 12 inches) and place one ball between the two sheets. Set aside the other ball for the top crust.

6. On the cutting board or table, gently roll the ball out into a circle. Push the rolling pin across the crust in many different directions to smooth out all the lumps. Continue until the crust almost reaches the edges of the waxed paper.

7. Remove the top piece of waxed paper, and place the pie pan upside down on top of the crust.

8. Put your hand under the bottom piece of paper, and quickly flip over the pie pan and crust. Remove the other piece of waxed paper.

9. Center the crust in the pie pan, and break off any extra crust hanging over the edge. Use the extra crust to repair any cracks or holes. You can make a pretty edge by pressing it into a zigzag shape.

APPLE FILLING

What You'll Need

- 2 or 3 apples

- 1/3 cup sugar

- 1 tablespoon vanilla

- 1 teaspoon lemon juice

- a knife or an apple corer/slicer, which cores and cuts six slices with one push through the apple. These gadgets are available at grocery and kitchen stores. Fancy kitchen stores sometimes sell the White Mountain Apple Corer, Peeler, Slicer Machine. You put the apple on a spit. When you crank the handle, this old-fashioned tool peels, slices, and cores it all at once!

- a bowl. Use the one you used for the crust, to save on cleaning.

- a spoon

What to Do

1. Core and slice the apples. You can peel them too, but you might want to try leaving the peels on—your pie will still taste great! Put the apples in the bowl.

2. Add the sugar, vanilla, and lemon juice, and mix.

3. Pour everything into the bottom crust.

TOP CRUST

1. Turn the oven on to 325°F (165°C).

2. Roll out the second ball of crust dough between two sheets of wax paper, and lay it over the apples in the pan. Decorate it in your own style. You can cut out designs in the crust or add extra crust pieces to make a pattern. Make at least some slits to let steam escape.

Yeah! Make this silly and easy top crust: Take a flour tortilla (medium or large size), and spread it with a little butter. Sprinkle it with sugar and cinnamon. Cut your own pattern into the tortilla, and put it over the apples.

3. Bake the pie for 20–25 minutes. Let it cool for at least 10 minutes.

4. Share the pie with your family. It will taste good! Or eat it all yourself—after all, *you made it!*

A Long Time Ago...

Here's a description of apple pies from 1758: "Apple-pie...is the evening meal of children. House-pie, in country places, is made of apples neither peeled nor freed from their cores, and its crust is not broken if a wagon wheel goes over it" (**Home Life in Colonial Days** by Alice Morse Earle, p. 146). I hope this doesn't describe **your** apple pie!

FANCY LEMONADE

★★

🕐 1 hour

This old-fashioned lemonade recipe takes a little while to make, but has a special taste because a yummy flavor comes out of the lemon peel.

What You'll Need

- 4 to 6 lemons (depending on size)
- 1 cup sugar
- 1 cup boiling water
- 2 cups ice
- 1 cup cold water
- a lemon squeezer
- a cup
- a large bowl

What to Do

1. Scrub the lemons clean.

2. Cut the lemons in half, and squeeze the juice into the cup.

3. Put the lemon peels in the bowl. Pour the sugar on them, stir, and leave for 1/2 hour.

4. With grown-up help, pour the boiling water on the peels, and stir to dissolve the sugar.

Caution: Get grown-up help with the boiling water—it is very hot and will burn your skin.

5. Mix in the ice, lemon juice, and cold water. (You can leave the lemon peels in the drink.) Taste the lemonade, and add more sugar or water if needed.

FULL MOON ADVENTURES

Nowadays we have electric lights and TV to keep us busy indoors at night. Sometimes we forget how beautiful and peaceful the natural world is at night. Try some nighttime adventures—just remember to take a grown-up, a flashlight, and reflective clothing.

SUNSET-MOONRISE PICNIC

★

🕐 As long as you want

Invite your family and friends to a picnic in a nice open spot with good views both east and west. Plan the picnic for the day of the full moon. Look on your calendar to find the date. Watch the sun set and the moon rise. If you don't have a lot of chances to be outside at night, it may surprise you to learn that the full moon rises as the sun sets.

SUNSET-MOONSET PICNIC

★

🕐 As long as you want

Plan another picnic for two weeks after the sunset-moonrise picnic, so you can watch the sliver of a moon set at almost the same time as the sun sets. Look at your calendar for the new moon (when it is totally invisible) and plan the party for the next evening. The moon will set right after the sun sets.

FULL-MOON WALK

★

🕐 **As long as you want**

When the moon is full, you can take a wonderful walk with your favorite grown-up. Bring a flashlight for safety, but try not to use it, so your eyes can get used to the soft moonlight. At first you will feel blind, but soon you will see!

Once upon a Time

Read **Walk When the Moon Is Full** by Frances Hamerstrom, a wonderful story about a family that takes a full-moon walk every month. Each time something different and magical happens. Ask your favorite grown-up to do monthly full-moon walks with you.

What to Do

- Look for owls. Listen for owls. Hoot to attract owls. You might be able to tiptoe up close to one.

- If you have a beaver pond nearby, you will have lots of fun, because beavers are nocturnal (active at night). You may see other nocturnal animals if you are lucky *and quiet*.

- If you are walking in a snowy landscape, you may be surprised at how very light it is. The snow reflects light. Sometimes just starlight and snow give enough illumination for you to see on a moonless night.

YARN PEOPLE

★★

🕐 30 minutes

A good time to be merry in the winter is Christmastime. Many North Country pioneers were originally from Scandinavia, and in Norway and Sweden people made yarn dolls to decorate Christmas trees. You can make bright red ones for your tree, or make some fun dolls just to play with. If the early settlers' kids had no yarn, they made this doll using dried grasses.

What You'll Need

- a ball of yarn
- (optional) scraps of cloth for doll clothes
- a paperback book or piece of cardboard 6 to 8 inches wide
- scissors
- (optional) a low-temperature glue gun

Caution: Get grown-up help. The glue comes out hot, and the tip of the gun is hot.

What to Do

1. Wind the yarn around the book or rectangle of cardboard at least 16 times, and cut the end.

2. Cut 7 short yarn ties, and use one to tie the strands together at the top (the doll's head).

3. Cut the yarn at the bottom, and remove the book or cardboard.

4. Tie the yarn strands 1 inch from the top to form the neck.

5. Separate 8 pieces of yarn for each arm, and trim a little off the arms so they don't hang down to the feet! Tie each arm at the wrist.

6. Tie the other 16 yarn pieces at the waist.

7. Trim the yarn evenly for the bottom of the skirt, or separate 8 pieces of yarn for each leg, and tie them at the ankle.

8. Make clothes for the doll if you like.

SNOWSTORM IN A BOTTLE

★

🕐 45 minutes

One thing for sure about the North Country is that the winters are long and snowy. Snow is sometimes seen as work by grown-ups, but kids know that snow is fun! In the early days, kids made wooden sleds. Nowadays you can blow up a huge truck inner tube and have a soft and fun ride. You can also make a snowstorm without getting cold—if you make it in a bottle.

What You'll Need

- a small or medium glass bottle with smooth sides, a wide mouth, and a tight lid. Check in your recycling box.

- enough water to fill your bottle

- a Styrofoam food tray. White ones are best.

- glitter and other kinds of "snow"

- scissors

- permanent pens

- a low-temperature glue gun or other waterproof glue

Caution: Get grown-up help. The glue comes out hot, and the tip of the gun is hot.

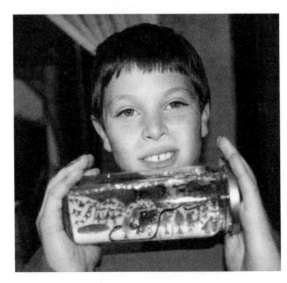

Fake Flakes

Can you make fake snow that will float down through water to look like real snowflakes? White plastic bread bag clasps cut into very tiny pieces work pretty well. Experiment with other "junk" you find around the house to see if it stays on top of the water, sinks quickly, or floats down slowly like real snowflakes.

1. Slide the foam back into the jar of glittery water, and screw the lid on carefully and securely.

2. Turn the bottle over, and make it snow.

What to Do

1. Cut a rectangle out of the smooth part of the Styrofoam food tray so that it fits into your glass bottle. Some Styrofoam has a waffle texture on the bottom, so use the smooth parts on the sides.

2. Draw a scene on the foam with the permanent pens. (Use these pens in a well-ventilated place, such as outdoors.) You can draw with the foam

rectangle upright (good for snowmen and tall mountains) or sideways (good for villages). Draw another scene on the back of the foam.

3. Glue the bottom of the picture onto the inside of the bottle lid.

Oops! You may think you are gluing the picture upside down, but the jar is not going to be upright; it will sit with the lid down or on its side.

4. Fill the bottle with water, and place the lid on top, so that the foam piece goes into the water, but don't screw the lid on. Let the extra water displaced by the foam drain out.

5. Take off the lid with the foam attached, and add glitter and other "snow" to the water.

Hain't Much, but You're Welcome to It: Southern Country Roots

SOUTHERNERS ARE FAMOUS for their hospitality. Even when they don't have much money, they know how to make a lot out of what they have, and they are very generous with it. When I lived in the Kentucky mountains and visited other families, they always wanted to feed me. They would cover their big kitchen tables with bowl after bowl and platter after platter of food and then quietly remark: "Hain't much, but you're welcome to it."

Amazing Mouth Bow

★★

🕐 30 minutes

This simple and fun device may be the world's first musical instrument. It is very, very old, from the Neolithic period (at least 4,000 years ago!), and seems to have been played all over the world, especially in Africa, Asia, and South America. Some Native American groups also played it. It was brought to the American South by slaves from Africa. In the old days a gourd was used as resonator. Later people used tin or aluminum cans. Now we use a plastic cup!

What You'll Need

- strong string

- a thin flexible stick, from 8 inches to 5 feet long. The traditional size is about 2 to 5 feet, but it is fun to make a small one too.

- a 1-cup yogurt container or plastic cup, for a resonator. Use flexible plastic (marked #1, #2, or #5), not hard plastic like #6, which is too tough to cut a slit in.

What to Do

1. Tie the string around one end of the stick. Then bend the stick, and tie the string to the other end to hold it bent. Ask a grown-up to help you make sure that the string is securely tied—you don't want it to snap in your face. You could put a nice big dab of hot glue on the knot to make it secure, or tie the string below a knob on the stick that will hold the string in place as shown in the illustration.

2. Make a slit near the lip of the plastic cup, and poke one end of the mouth bow in it.

3. Put the other end in your mouth. You can hold it in your teeth, but keep your mouth open so the sound isn't squelched. Now pluck the string while you bend the stick more and unbend it to change the note. Isn't that cool?

Singing

It doesn't take money to make music. Among the poor people in the American South, singing was and is an important part of life. When slaves were forced to work long hours in the fields, they communicated with others nearby using a musical field holler. "They sang about things like pain, agony, and death. They also sang about love, justice, and mercy. The slaves had nothing but their belief in God, and so they sang about that a lot. If you visited a slave gathering, you would probably hear them singing songs that would reach right down into your soul" **(Kids Explore America's African-American Heritage** by the Westridge Young Writers Workshop, p. 54).

Musical Jugs

★

🕐 15 minutes

Mountaineer jug bands and old-time African-American street bands have much in common. They both have been making music for almost a hundred years. They both use very interesting combinations of instruments made out of found objects: jugs, washboards, washtubs, hubcaps, kazoos, combs, cans, frying pans, spoons, hoe blades, cowbells, whistles, and bicycle pumps!

What You'll Need

- glass bottles from juice, sparkling cider, root beer, or maple syrup
- enough water to fill the bottles

What to Do

1. Blow across the top of each bottle to see what sounds you get.

2. Add water to make a higher sound.

3. Line up a bunch of bottles with different sounds, and try playing a tune!

Amazing Grace Notes

The religious singing of the hill people in the Appalachian Mountains has a hauntingly beautiful sound when it floats across the mountains. Since many mountain folk couldn't read, they didn't use hymn books. Instead, they had one person "line out" the words at the beginning of each line, fitting it into the short break between lines. The group then sang the words, stretching them out and adding lots of improvised grace notes.

Once upon a Time

To get a good idea of what life was like in the South around the time of slavery, check out **A Picture of Freedom: The Diary of Clotee, a Slave Girl** by Patricia C. McKissack.

Party Ideas

To hear what this happy, energetic music sounds like, ask your local music store for recordings of the Memphis Jug Band and Cannon's Jug Stompers from the 1920s, the Jim Kweskin Jug Band, and the Even Dozen Jug Band from the 1960s.

African Drums

★

🕐 **30 minutes**

Most slaves were not allowed to play drums, even though drumming had been an important part of their African culture. After slavery was abolished, African-Americans joyfully reclaimed this great way to make music.

What You'll Need

- a round container (from oatmeal, coffee, hot chocolate, etc.), made of cardboard, plastic, or metal, with a plastic lid. If you tear the paper label off some coffee containers, you'll have a shiny silver drum.

- a pencil with an eraser end, for a drumstick

- sticky paper (contact paper, shelf lining, stickers)

- (optional) paint (tempera or acrylic)

- (optional) cloth or pretty paper

- (optional) a low-temperature glue gun or white glue

Caution: Get grown-up help. The glue comes out hot, and the tip of the gun is hot.

What to Do

1. Tap your container with your hands or the eraser end of the pencil to see if it has a nice sound. Find one that does.

2. Decorate the sides of the drum.

   - For any kind of container: use sticky paper.

   - For a cardboard container: use white glue to attach pretty cloth or paper, or use tempera paint.

   - For a plastic or metal container: use a low-temperature glue gun to attach pretty cloth or paper, or use acrylic paint.

3. Join a band.

Stomp Dances

Circle dancing around a sacred fire is an ancient tradition intended to bring the dancers back in balance with the world. These dances are still enjoyed by the Cherokee, Creek, Seminole, and Shawnee tribes of the Southeast. Everyone dances to the music, while the men and boys sing, and the women and girls make rhythms with rattles tied to their legs. These rattles are called **shackles** and are traditionally made of hollow turtle shells with pebbles inside. Nowadays they are sometimes made with tin cans and pebbles.

Storytelling

★

🕐 **Hours and hours, if you want**

In the evening, when work is done, it's fun to sit out on the back porch and tell stories. In the days before television, southern mountain people ate dinner early so they could go visiting. Adults and kids would tell stories and laugh far into the night.

What to Do

- **Your Turn:** You start a story, about any old thing, and talk till you run out of ideas. End with "and suddenly—" The next person goes on from there. You'll probably have a very silly, fun time.

- **Part Two: The Return of…:** Read a good story from one of the southern cultures, and then add on to it.

- **Trickster Tales:** Africans who were brought to the United States as slaves managed to create a rich culture of songs, jokes, riddles, and tales, even in the middle of extreme hardship. One of their most wonderful characters is Brer or Bruh (meaning Brother) Rabbit. Even though he is small and always getting into trouble, he outsmarts the other

characters in the story in very satisfying ways. You can probably think of some tricks for Brer Rabbit to try.

- **Tall Tales:** "Hornswoggle" comes from the Kentucky mountain men, who loved to tell tall tales and make up wild words. It means to bamboozle, swindle, cheat, defraud, hoax. You and your friends can tell tall tales. Think of an adventurous thing you have done and tell a story that exaggerates what you did. How many amazing stories can you invent?

- **Haunt Tales:** The Appalachian hill people love to tell scary stories. You can tell scary stories. I hope you won't make yourself too scared to sleep!

Once upon a Time

Richard Chase has collected mountain tales in two books: **Grandfather Tales** and **The Jack Tales.**

You might be surprised at how similar some Cherokee and African-American stories are! These two cultures obviously respected and learned from each other. Read "Doc Rabbit, Bruh Fox, and Tar Baby" in **The People Could Fly: American Black Folktales** by Virginia Hamilton, and then read "Rabbit and the Tar Wolf" in **How Rabbit Tricked Otter and Other Cherokee Trickster Stories** by Gayle Ross.

57

Sticks and Staffs

★

🕐 1 hour

The American South has cultural influences from Africa, Europe, and the indigenous peoples. African-Americans came from west and central Africa, where decorated ceremonial staffs were common, often adorned with serpents. It turns out that the Europeans and Native Americans also decorated their walking sticks and staffs with serpents.

What You'll Need

- a stick about 3 to 6 feet tall. If you can't find one in your backyard, ask your neighbors. If someone nearby is having a tree pruned, ask for a branch the right size.

- yarn

- pretty things to attach: feathers, fur, yarn, colorful cloth strips, ribbons, bells, string

- scissors

- glue

What to Do

1. Wrap parts of the stick with yarn or cloth.

2. Attach decorations to any part of the stick by tying or gluing them on. Attach some things by dangling them from pieces of yarn and ribbons tied to the stick.

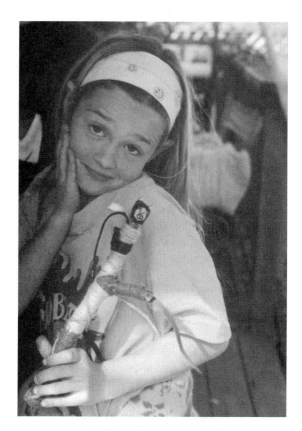

A Long Time Ago...

Here are some old-time decorated sticks that are fun to make and might be useful to solve problems that you may come across in your life.

African Spokesperson's Staff: In some African villages, the person who has the experience and good judgment to solve problems and help the group to work well together carries this staff. You and your friends can use a similar idea when you meet as a group. If you have a problem with people interrupting and not listening to what others have to say, give the spokesperson's staff to the person who has the right to speak. When that person is done, she or he hands the staff to the next person who wants to talk.

Owner Stick: Some Native American groups used a stick to mark ownership of items such as hides or firewood. It was simpler to place a unique signature stick next to the item than to have to tell everyone that it was yours. Maybe you can use an owner stick to mark a plate of cookies that you are too full to finish now but plan to eat later. If you leave your owner stick protecting the goodies, someone else won't think you didn't want them! Be sure to explain exactly what the funny-looking stick means. Your family will quickly learn (and want sticks of their own)!

Walking Stick: Europeans liked to carve wooden walking sticks for their travels in the wild. When they came to the southern mountains of the United States, they brought their love of carving with them. Carving is a wonderful, inexpensive art, because all you need is a knife and some wood from the forest. If you live where the mountains are steep, make yourself a walking stick to lean on and pull yourself uphill. It will also help keep you from falling as you go down steep, slippery slopes.

Big Bold African Jewelry

★ ★

🕐 1 hour

Many people in Africa traditionally wore beautiful bright, flowing clothes and amazing jewelry. You can feel lots of pride when you make Big Bold African Jewelry.

What You'll Need

- jewel-like materials that might normally get thrown away: rocks, shells, aluminum foil, and other foil candy wrappings

- sewing leftovers: velvety or shiny cloth, rickrack, lace, fancy buttons, sequins, yarn

- unusual things that can look quite wonderful when used for jewelry: keys, bottle caps, small tiles, Styrofoam packing curlicues, confetti, glitter, old stamps, metal clasps from manila envelopes, samples of countertop material from hardware stores or home improvement centers (they are about 1-1/2 by 2-1/2 inches, with a convenient hole at one end)

- beads

- for necklaces: telephone wire, regular wire, yarn, bread twist ties, and wires that were wrapped around vegetables. You can strip off the paper.

- for bracelets: cardboard tubes that are wide enough for your hand to go into (about 2 inches across). Some kinds of tape come on wide tubes (they work perfectly when they are empty). You can cut a long poster mailing tube into 2-inch sections with grown-up help.

- for decorating: stickers, shelf-lining paper, pens, and pencils

- a low-temperature glue gun

Caution: Get grown-up help. The glue comes out hot, and the tip of the gun is hot.

What to Do

1. Make big bold necklaces.

- Look through your materials for things that have holes for stringing. Telephone wire is easiest to use for stringing beads, because it pokes through the smallest holes and does not get caught the way string or yarn does. Any bead that the wire won't go through can be saved to glue onto a bracelet.

- Glue various beautiful things to countertop samples that you've strung on your necklace.

- Twist the wire ends of the necklace into loops. Tie a piece of yarn through each loop, so that you can fasten the necklace with a soft yarn bow at the back of your neck.

2. Make big bold bracelets. Attach wonderful things to your cardboard tubes, using the glue gun. Or use stickers, shelf-lining paper, pens, and pencils to decorate the tubes.

Hobby Horfe

★★

🕐 1 hour

Making a stick horse with a sock is fun and easy. Sometimes the seam at the toe of the sock looks just like a smiling mouth.

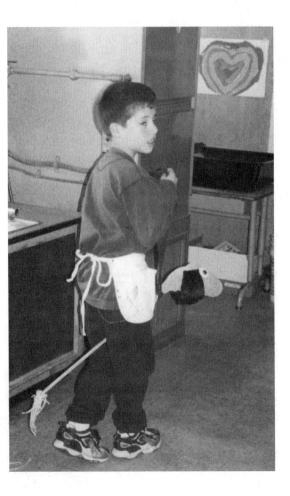

What You'll Need

- a sock. Here's a use for that single sock that has lost its mate!

- stuffing. Use pillow or quilt stuffing or pieces of soft cloth.

- a stick about 1 yard long. Try to find a fairly straight, smooth one. An old broom handle is really good. Have a grown-up cut off any extra length.

- yarn

- buttons or beads for eyes

- furry cloth for ears

- string or rope for reins

- colored pens to draw on features

- a low-temperature glue gun

Caution: Get grown-up help. The glue comes out hot, and the tip of the gun is hot.

- (optional) thread and a needle

A Long Time Ago...

The idea of making a fake horse to ride comes from England. Some of the people in the southern mountains were originally from England. They moved to isolated valleys (called "hollers"), and kept many of their English traditions. The hobby horse was originally part of a dance play in which one character rode a fake horse made from a sort of basket covered with hide or cloth and worn around the waist, so that people legs were pretend horse legs.

62

What to Do

1. Stuff the sock half way.

2. Slip the sock on the stick and stuff around the stick so that the horse's head is at right angles to the stick. Tie the sock in place with yarn. You may need grown-up help making it secure.

3. Glue or sew on the eyes and the ears.

4. Glue on a yarn mane, and braid it. Glue or tie on the string or rope for reins.

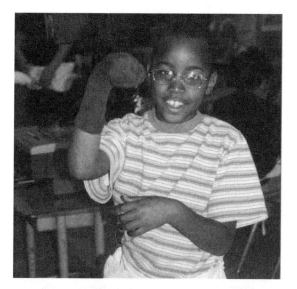

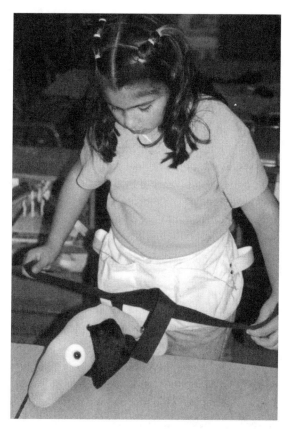

Hair Today

★

🕐 As long as you want

What You'll Need

- Some Hair!

What to Do

- Do you know how to braid hair? It is pretty simple. Just divide the hair (or yarn, if you're braiding your hobby horse's mane) into three sections. Put the one on the left over to the middle, then put the one on the right over to the middle. Keep doing this till you get to the end.

- Cornrowing is not so simple! This beautiful African-inspired hairstyle has lots of skinny braids. Kids these days wear wonderful, fun cornrow styles with hair extensions and added beads that take hours to complete. It feels so good to have someone spend lots of time making you beautiful. Cornrowing is done differently from braiding. Start by dividing a small amount of hair into three strands. Braid the strands, but each time you put one section over the other, gather up a little more hair from right next to the braid. The cornrow should lie flat on the head. As you braid a cornrow, you can overlap the strands as described above, or you can put the left strand *under* to the middle, then the right *under* to the middle.

Party Ideas

Get some friends together, and try braiding each other's hair. Do part of their hair overhand and part underhand. See if it looks different, if one sticks out and the other lies flat.

Fun Facts

Some early Native American men of the Southeast, the Muskhogeans, wore their hair sticking up in front in a "roach" with braided "lovelocks" on either side and a "scalp lock" pulled through a hair tube hanging behind. The rest of the hair was cut very short or plucked. Maybe the unusual hairstyles that some people sport today are not so new after all!

Small Dolls

★

⏱ **30 minutes**

All over the world for a very long time, dolls have been made by kids and for kids out of found materials. You can make really cute dolls out of clothespins, corks, wooden spools, and Popsicle sticks.

What You'll Need

- a bunch of different things to put together into a doll, such as

- clothespins (old-fashioned all-wood pegs are best, but the newer kind with a spring also work), corks (from wine or champagne), Popsicle sticks, wooden thread spools, wooden beads, old Velcro, old socks, and old yarn (for hair!), wire (pipe cleaners, telephone wire, or vegetable wires), yarn, cloth

- a serrated knife to cut the cork if necessary

- colored pencils or fine-tip felt pens

- a low-temperature glue gun

Caution: Get grown-up help. The glue comes out hot, and the tip of the gun is hot.

Homemade Toys and Dolls

All toys were homemade until the time of the industrial revolution, which happened around in America after the Civil War in 1865. Middle class people started buying toys, but poor people in America continued to make toys out of what they found around. Now toys are so inexpensive that most people can buy them. But homemade toys are lots of fun to make and then to play with!

Save the Earth

You can unravel socks to get curly hair. If you have short pieces of Velcro, either the wooly or the hook side can be used for hair.

What to Do

There are many ways to make these dolls.

1. Decide what kind of doll you want to make. You can use a wooden bead for the head and make a body out of a clothespin, a cork, or an empty thread spool. You can also make the whole doll out of a clothespin, a cork, or a popsicle stick. For ideas, look at all the wonderful kinds of dolls that other kids have made.

2. Use the colored pencils or fine-tip felt pens to draw a delicate face. Glue on the hair.

3. If you want arms on your doll, make them with wire.

4. Draw or paint clothes onto the body, or make them out of cloth.

Fun Facts

One very famous African-American was Dr. George Washington Carver. Born a slave, he educated himself and became a scientist. He developed 300 uses for peanuts(!) so that poor southerners (both blacks and whites) would have a crop to grow that would make them a better living.

Some old-fashioned dolls were made of peanuts! You can make a doll out of six peanuts in their shells. Use one peanut for the head and chest, so draw a face on the top half. Use one for the hips, two for the legs, and two for the arms, and glue them all together. Put a dress on the strange body to cover it, and you have a doll!

"You'll Never Be Bored" Board Game

★ ★

🕐 1–2 hours

Every culture seems to have board games that children and grown-ups deeply love. Some games are ancient, and some are pretty new. If you have never made up a board game, you are in for a lot of fun.

What You'll Need

- for the board: a cardboard box or flat packaging piece of cardboard

- for the pieces: metal and plastic bottle tops, tops from squirt bottles, corks, pieces from old games, marbles, and beans

- for the cards: heavy paper, thin cardboard, and old decks of cards

- for dice: cubes of wood or foam or old dice from another game

- for decorations: any kind of small interesting pieces of wood, paper, and plastic

- plain stickers or labels

- colored pens, pencils, crayons

- a low temperature glue gun, white glue, or glue sticks

Caution: Get grown-up help. The glue comes out hot, and the tip of the gun is hot.

What to Do

1. Look at all the things that you have collected, and start to imagine what game you could make with them. You can create games for a flat board with cards and pieces and a path to follow, like Monopoly or Clue. You might make a more three-dimensional game like Mousetrap. You might even want to make a physical game like Twister. Of course, your game will be totally unique and quite wonderful.

2. Make the rules. One of the challenging aspects of making a game is thinking of the rules. A good game gives everyone an equal chance to win. Most games involve some strategy, although some games are purely luck (like Snakes and Ladders). A game based on luck can be quite hilarious. There is something satisfying about not being responsible for the outcome. A game based on strategy is harder to design. But you may be surprised—your own game might be more challenging than you imagined. Maybe you'll design a game that's cooperative rather than competitive, where winning depends on working together.

3. Make pieces. You could cut the king's and queen's heads from an old deck of cards and glue them onto corks or bottle tops to make players. You can name your pieces: the top of the mustard squirt bottle could be Mr. Mustard, the top to the shampoo bottle could be Priscilla Pert.

4. Make dice cubes from wood or foam. The foam ones bounce in a fun way. Write numbers on the six sides. Or draw a color on each side that relates to the game in some way—for instance, if you throw the dice and it lands with the orange side up, you can jump to the next orange square on the board.

5. Make the cards. Many games have cards that you draw when you land on certain squares. The cards you make for your game can be as silly as you want. Be sure to make some good luck cards and some bad luck cards.

6. Play the game. You'll need to play it several times to figure out what changes to make in the rules or in the board design. You might need more safe spots—or more hazards. When you make a game, you never know if it will take five minutes for someone to win or five hours! In any case, it's a lot of fun to play home-made games. They are usually quite hilarious. Maybe your game will be so wonderful that you could sell it and make enough money to pay for college.

Tenderfeet and Greenhorns: The California Gold Rush

STARTING IN 1848 with the discovery of gold near Sutter's Mill, loads of people left their homes to come to California and make their fortune (or not). Most of them had no experience mining or traveling in the wilderness, but they were amazingly resourceful. They made it to California and then began the hard work of mining. These folks may have been "tenderfeet" and "greenhorns" (new to the rigors of pioneering and mining), but they survived.

It was hard to get to California. You could sail around the tip of South America (which wasn't easy) or sail to Panama and then go overland through the jungle (which was even harder). Instead, a lot of people crossed the wild continent in wagon trains. Pioneers had traveled across the country before this, but the route to California was still unmapped. So many people headed across that they created America's first traffic jam!

Who Came to the Gold Rush?

- Men (and not very many women) from all over the world. At first everyone got along well; the miners helped each other and didn't steal. Later the drifters, gamblers, swindlers, desperadoes, and cutthroats came.

- California natives were already here. Many were forced to work for low wages, or were paid with nothing but food and clothes in the gold rush. The 1800s were a terrible time for native people, but they managed to preserve their culture. Each fall, even today, they hold a fall festival celebrating the acorn harvest. They share their good food and encourage visitors to join with them in some of their traditional dances. The dancing continues far into the night around the magical light of the fire. For more information, call (209) 296-7488.

- Chinese men came to California in the gold rush. Luckily, they brought much-needed food to sell to the hungry miners, as well as cloth, tools, and even prefabricated houses! Nevertheless they were treated with prejudice and had to work extra hard to succeed.

- African-Americans came to find gold, and many prospered. Some were from the northern states and were already free, but some came as slaves with their owners. The California Underground Railroad helped to free many of them.

- South Americans, Mexicans, and Californios also became miners. Californios were Spanish people who had come to California before the gold rush to raise cattle.

- One-fifth of the miners were from France. They were called Keskydees because they kept saying, **"Qu'est-ce qu'il dit"** (pronounced "Kess-keel-dee"), which means "What did he say?" in French.

- The Australian government sent its worst convicts to California to get rid of them!

- Hawaiians and other South Sea Islanders had been trading with California for a while, and they didn't want to miss out on the chance to get rich.

Fun Facts

Gold fever produced some strange bargains offered to the people heading out to the gold fields.

One "invention" was a grease that would make gold and nothing else stick to your body. You would just roll down a hill and stand up rich!

Another "invention" was a huge balloon "Aerial Locomotive." While it was still in the planning stages, the inventor signed up several hundred people and told them the trip to California would take only three days! Reality set in when he realized his idea wouldn't fly.

Pouch for Precious Things

★★

🕐 1 hour

Gold rush miners carried their gold with them. They tied long, narrow leather pouches to their belts. Some California natives (and others) carried their gold in a hollow bird's quill attached to a leather necklace. A wooden peg was used to close the top, and a leather holder protected the quill from breaking. You can make a pouch that goes around your neck or one that ties to your belt loop. You might want to use it as a good-luck or plan-ahead pouch and fill it with found objects (such as rocks and crystals), medicine objects (such as herbs and Band-Aids), and useful objects (such as erasers, hair ties, and spending money).

Fun Fact

Miners' pants had pockets, but they got worn and torn by the weight of the gold in them. For cash they used gold dust—one pinch was worth one dollar—so they carried their "money" around in pouches. During the height of the gold rush, prices were ridiculously inflated—a dollar for a piece of bread! Even now, 150 years later, you wouldn't want to pay that.

It Didn't Always Pan Out

Panning for gold was supposed to be easy: just fill a pan with water and "pay dirt" (sandy soil from the stream), and then swish it until the gold, which is eight times heavier, falls to the bottom. If the miners couldn't get the pan that was specially designed for gold, they used their fry pans or washbowls or even Indian baskets made of tightly woven grass. Sometimes they just used a pocket knife and spoons to dig out pockets of gold dust, and a blanket to shake the dirt so that the lighter stuff blew away and left the gold. Surprisingly, these simple methods did make some people very rich. But usually a miner had to go through about a ton of sand to get an ounce of gold.

Native American Medicine Pouches

Some Native American groups used pouches to hold their medicines. Some medicines were herbs, and some were believed to have magical or spiritual properties. The leaves of bay laurel trees and manzanita bushes were used for medicine by California natives.

FOR A LACED POUCH

What You'll Need

- tracing paper

- 2 pieces of leather about 3 by 4 inches. You can buy leather at a hobby store or use fake leather vinyl.

- a leather thong or shoelace 1 to 1-1/2 feet long for a pocket pouch or 3 feet long for a necklace pouch.

- a bead with a large hole or a shank button (a button shaped like a mushroom with a hole in the stem)

- scissors

- a hammer and a nail, or an awl, or a hole punch. An awl is a leather-working tool that looks like a nail with a handle.

- a block of wood at least 3 by 4 inches

- a pencil

What to Do

1. Trace the pouch pattern shown in the illustration. Cut out your tracing-paper pattern.

2. Using the pattern, cut two pieces of leather for each pouch.

3. Put the two pieces together, right sides out.

4. Use the block of wood to protect your table. Using the hammer and nail (or awl or hole punch), make holes about 1/2 inch apart around the edge of the two layers of leather.

5. Poke a pencil through the holes to widen them.

6. Lace the leather thong through the two layers, in and out, around the pouch.

7. Even out the ends of the thong, and slip the bead over the two ends. Push the bead down to the pouch to hold it closed.

8. Tie the ends of the thong, and put it on!

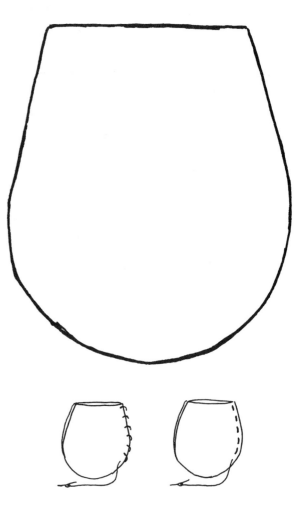

74

FOR A SEWN POUCH

What You'll Need

- all the materials for a laced pouch

- dental floss and a regular needle, or yarn and a yarn needle—a needle with a wide enough eye for yarn to go through

What to Do

1. Follow steps 1–2 for a laced pouch.

2. Put the pieces of leather together, right sides in.

3. Sew around the sides and bottom of your pouch with the floss or yarn, using the in and out (running) stitch, or the looping over (blanket) stitch (see the illustrations). Knot your ends strongly. You may need grown-up help with this step.

Oops! If you are a beginner at hand sewing, use the blanket stitch, because it is easier to keep the stitches near the edge. With the running stitch you might sew too far from the edge. (The running stitch does makes a good seam for the pouch, if you are good at sewing, because, if you pull the stitches tight as you sew, they

form a kind of zigzag seam that is really pretty.

4. Turn the pouch right side out.

5. Make four holes in the top of the pouch with the hammer and nail or awl or hole punch, using the block of wood to protect your table. Poke the pencil through the holes to widen them.

6. Thread the leather thong through the holes. Put the bead on the thong, slide it down to close the pouch, and tie the ends of the thong.

7. You can glue or sew on beads, fur, and feathers to make your pouch extra beautiful.

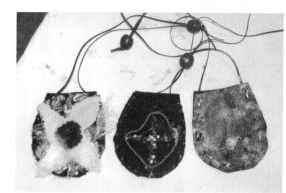

Old Jeans Backpack

★★★

🕐 1–1/2 hours

Blue jeans were invented for the gold rush because prospecting was such hard work that regular pants would wear out in no time. Mr. Levi Strauss had brought some material for tents and wagon covers, but he found that what people needed was strong pants. After he used up all his canvas to make pants, he bought strong blue material from Nîmes, France. ("Of Nîmes" = *de Nîmes* = denim!) Pants made of the blue denim quickly became very popular. They have been popular ever since and are worn all over the world. Miners were so low on supplies that some made bags out of their old jeans, tying the legs and using the jeans to carry the **pay dirt.** I guess these were the first blue jeans backpacks!

What You'll Need

- 1 pair of old worn jeans. Use any size—they all make good packs.

- an old pair of suspenders, or 2 old cloth belts, ties, or other strong cloth strips for shoulder straps

- a piece of rope or a wide shoestring for the drawstring that closes the pack

- scissors

- a tape measure or yardstick

- straight pins

- a sewing machine, thread, and grown-up help

- permanent pens or fabric paints

- (optional) yarn, safety pins, and little things to hang off your pack

What to Do

1. Cut the legs off the jeans by cutting straight across at the crotch. (Take them off first!) Cut through the crotch seam so you have one continuous opening for the bottom of the pack (like a very short skirt).

2. Use material from one of the cut-off legs for the bottom of the pack. Cut off the cuff, then measure about 15 inches up the leg, and cut across the leg. You now have a cylinder of cloth, which will form the double-thick bottom of the backpack.

3. Pin the double-thick bottom piece in place. Get grown-up help lining it up. It doesn't have to fit exactly—it's OK for the cloth to end up with folds or puckers.

Oops! Be sure to put the right side of the jeans in, so the seam will be on the inside (see the illustration).

4. Have a grown-up help you use the sewing machine. The grown-up could sew the two short sides of the bottom into place. Once those are sewn, you can remove the pins.

Caution: Sewing machines are a little dangerous. Keep your fingers away from the rapidly moving needle. If you have never sewn with a machine, start by dividing the work. First you can learn to gently push the power pedal, while your grown-up helper guides the fabric through. Then you can steer the fabric through as your helper gently pushes the power pedal. Eventually you will be able to do both at once, and not sew your fingers!

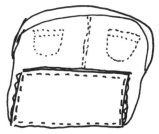

5. Once the two short seams are sewn, the two long sides of the bottom are pretty easy to sew. It doesn't matter if you don't do it perfectly, and it's OK to gather some material to make the pieces fit. After you sew the seam, turn the bag right side out, and you'll never have to think about that seam again!

6. Have a grown-up help you sew on the pack straps. You can sew them to either the zipper side or the pocket side of the jeans. Which side of the pack do you want to have showing when you wear it? Sew the tops of the straps to the middle of the jeans waistband. Then try on the pack to measure where to place the bottom ends of the straps. You can sew them kitty-corner on the bottom of the pack (see the illustration). Sew the seams across several times to make them strong.

7. Now decorate the pack with drawings done in permanent pens or fabric paints. You can also tie or safety pin decorations on.

8. Loop a rope or wide shoestring through the belt loops to cinch up your pack.

9. Fill up your pack with food, water, and a good book, and take a hike! But don't weigh yourself down with too many schoolbooks or too much gold!

Off the Cuff

Make a sailor hat! Take a look at the picture on page 12.

78

Sourdough Pancakes

★ ★

🕐 1 hour

You may not work as hard as the miners did, but you still probably wake up hungry. These pancakes make a yummy start to the day.

What You'll Need

- sourdough starter in a glass or plastic container
- a ceramic or glass bowl
- 1 cup flour
- 1 cup water
- 2 eggs
- 1 cup milk
- 1 cup pancake mix
- oil or butter to grease the griddle
- a 1/3-cup measuring scoop
- an electric pancake griddle or a fry pan and stove
- a spatula

San Francisco Sourdough Bread

It is made with only flour, water, salt, and starter, yet it is the world's most famous sourdough bread. Why? Two factors affect the taste: the particular wild yeast that thrives in the Bay Area and the way of baking the bread in a steamy brick oven. You can't duplicate it, so you just have to come to San Francisco to eat some. If you want to try making it, the recipe is in **Jake O'Shaughnessey's Sourdough Book** by Timothy Firnstahl.

Sourdough Starter

Sourdough is a batter full of wild yeast. Back in the early days, people made their own starter. You might want to try to catch your own yummy wild yeast by mixing 1 cup flour and 1 cup water in a glass or plastic container and leaving it out of the refrigerator for a week or so. Be sure to have a grown-up check that it is not rotten before you cook with it! It will smell spicy (good) or moldy and rotten (bad). The safest way for modern kids to get a sourdough starter is to ask for some from a friend who has a starter or to buy powdered starter from a gourmet grocery store or cooking store. Once you have a starter going, keep it in the refrigerator until you are ready to cook with it. To keep it working right, use it to make pancakes about once a week.

What to Do

1. The evening before you want pancakes, take the starter jar out of the refrigerator, and pour the starter into the ceramic or glass bowl. Add the flour and water, and let the mixture "work" (bubble and grow) in a warm spot all night.

2. In the morning, take 1 cup of starter out of the bowl. Put the rest back in your jar, and save it for next time in the refrigerator.

3. Put the cup of starter back in the bowl, and add the eggs, milk, and pancake mix. Stir well.

4. With grown-up help, heat your griddle or pan to 350°F (175°C). Grease it with the oil or butter.

5. Use the 1/3 cup measuring scoop to pour batter onto the hot griddle. Make as many pancakes as will fit without crowding. Watch them cook. When bubbles form on the top, the pancakes are ready to turn. If you are cooking on a griddle, you have to turn them with a regular old spatula.

80

Flapjack Flipping

★★

🕐 30 minutes

Have you ever heard pancakes called *flap-jacks*? They are called that because one way to turn them over is to cook a pan-size one and then flip it over in the air and catch it in the pan. In England people celebrate something called "Pancake Day," where they see who can flip the biggest one and not drop it! It is part of a much older Christian tradition that involves eating pancakes, because flour is the staff of life, milk represents inno-cence, and eggs symbolize rebirth.

What You'll Need

- oil or butter to grease the pan
- a batch of pancake batter
- a small fry pan and stove
- a spatula
- a 1/3-cup measuring scoop
- a hot pad

What to Do

1. With grown-up help, heat your pan to 350°F (175°C). Grease it with the oil or butter, and put in a scoop of bat-ter.

2. Cook until the top has little bubbles.

3. Shake the pan to make sure the pancake is loose. Use the spatula to loosen it if necessary.

4. Then hold the pan with a hot pad, and give a jerking-forward-and-up movement. The pancake should flip in the air. Catch the pancake in the pan. (Practice with a cool pan and an already-made pancake. You will become an expert in no time.)

Fun Fact

Prices really soared during the gold rush. It was a little expensive to make these pancakes when eggs cost $10 to $50 a dozen, butter cost $6 a pound, and flour cost $800 a barrel. When miners couldn't afford those prices, they had to make their pancakes with just flour, sourdough starter, and water.

Have you heard of hoecakes? They're corn pancakes. Early Americans some-times baked them over a campfire, on the metal part of a hoe (a tool usually used for weeding gardens)!

Patent Medicines

★

🕐 **30 minutes**

Many of the medicines sold to the gold miners were quack (phony) remedies. The makers claimed all kinds of fantastic cures, but actually the medicines had little or no value in fighting or curing disease. The gold miners did get sick, and they spent some of their hard-earned money to buy patent medicines. One English gold miner said it was an American characteristic to imbibe quack remedies in huge quantities: "They dosed themselves with all the medicines they could get hold of, so that when they really were taken ill, they were already half poisoned with the stuff they had been swallowing" (*Gold Fever* by George W. Groh, p. 41). You can have fun making pretend pills, creams, and elixirs. (An elixir is a drink that is supposed to make you live a long time.) Remember, these are all just pretend!

What You'll Need

- small bottles, empty and clean, from shampoo samples, flavoring extracts, or real medicines
- small containers with lids
- beads, pebbles, Styrofoam pellets cut into tiny pieces
- flour
- food coloring, or pieces of colored tissue paper soaked in water to create dye
- labels
- pens

Caution: Absolutely, definitely, do *not* eat this medicine! And don't try to trick your little siblings into taking it—they may be too young to understand that it is a joke. This is IMPORTANT!

Party Idea

Try making Patent Medicine at your next slumber party.

What to Do

- Gather all your materials, and see what kinds of medicines you are inspired to make. Look at some of the photos to get ideas.

- Make creams by combining flour, water, and food coloring or tissue-paper dye.

- Make pills with beads, pebbles, and pellets.

- Make liquid elixirs that will cure all people's problems.

- Label your remedies with claims and directions.

Here are some medicines that kids have made:

- School Excuse Pills: Take one, and it will help you think of a very convincing excuse for not doing your homework, being late, or chewing gum in class.

- Slumber Pills for Kids: Will *not* let you fall asleep. Extremely useful for slumber parties. Take 1 per slumber party.

- Wish Elixir: Keep out of reach of grown-ups. Very flammable! Directions: Breathe on the mixture. Will start to froth. Make a wish, it will be answered.

- Instant Maid: Soak one pill in water and a maid will appear. Only works for 2 hours. Keep out of reach of parents.

- Instant Cold: Gives you a horrible cough but you will feel fine. Allows you to miss 3 days of school before taking another pill.

Fun Fact

You may be surprised to find out that Coca-Cola started out as a patent medicine. The syrup was invented in 1886 to cure headaches, exhaustion, and nervousness. By mistake fizzy water was added to the syrup, and then the makers discovered how good it tasted that way!

Root Beer

★ ★ ★

🕐 **1 hour**

For an elixir that you *can* drink, make some root beer! Root beer started out as a healthy hot tea that was good for the stomach. It was a Native American drink made of licorice, sassafras, and fennel. The European settlers loved it. It was even sold as a patent medicine. Today's root beer ingredients are more complicated, but it's still a popular drink, especially when combined with ice cream in a root beer float.

What You'll Need

- clean bottles from sparkling cider, champagne, or root beer, but not the kind with a screw-on lid

Caution: Be sure to use bottles that can withstand pressure. Bottles that contained carbonated beverages, such as soda or sparkling apple cider, will work. Wash the bottles thoroughly before starting the project.

- root beer supplies from a wine- and beer-making store: root beer extract, special yeast, new bottle caps, and a capper (a simple machine that secures the caps onto the bottles)

- water

- sugar

- a big pot

- a funnel

- a long-handled spoon

- a pouring cup

Party Idea

Invite your friends over, and try this experiment: Have each person make two root beer floats. In one, pour the root beer in the glass first, and then add a scoop of ice cream. In the other, put in a scoop of ice cream, and pour the root beer over it. Which one foams more?

Answer: The eruption is caused by the quick release of carbon dioxide from the root beer. Usually it bubbles out slowly, and the drink stays fizzy for a while, but the milky ice cream makes it come out more quickly and erupt. There may be less eruption when the ice cream is on top, because not all of the root beer has ice cream touching it. When the ice cream is put in first, all of the root beer ends up coming in contact with ice cream, which releases more carbon dioxide.

Be sure to eat the experiment! You may need to repeat the experiment to "check your results."

What to Do

- This project has parts that are hard to do. You will need grown-up help.

- The directions for mixing, bottling, and capping the root beer will come with the extract. Follow the directions exactly, especially those about the amount of yeast.

Oops! Too much yeast will create too much carbon dioxide, and the pressure will cause the bottle caps to come shooting off. That could be dangerous!

Your Own Private Label

★

🕐 30 minutes

It's really fun to make your own labels. You can label your homemade root beer or take the label off a commercial root beer and put your original label on.

What You'll Need

- plain stickers or paper
- pens, pencils, markers
- paste or tape

What to Do

Design a label using your own wonderful ideas. Look at the photos for some fun labels that other kids have made.

Lizards and Skulls: The American Southwest

THE NATIVE AMERICAN, Mexican, and cowboy cultures that thrive in the Southwest make up a spicy stew: all the parts interact to make a richer mix than the separate ingredients. Our recipe starts with a land that is beautiful, open, dry, and rugged, with only those plants and animals that can survive in a hot climate. From the mesas (high rock outcroppings, with tops as flat as tables), add the Hopi and other Pueblo people who have lived here longer than anyone in any other part of the United States. Next stir in the Navajos, who arrived around 1,000 years ago. Add the Spanish who came north from Mexico and the horses and sheep they brought. Now your Southwest stew is ready, full of cowboys, weavers, farmers, and the other diverse people of the Southwest.

Leaping Lizard

★★

🕐 1 hour

The Southwest is a great place for lizards to live. Lizards and snakes are cold-blooded, but that doesn't mean they are cold—it means that they are the same temperature as the air around them. When the air is cold, they cool down. When the weather is too hot, they hide from the sun to keep from overheating. Cold-blooded animals need less food to survive than warm-blooded ones. We burn food to keep our bodies at an even temperature. Since cold-blooded animals don't use their food to produce body heat, they can go much longer without food. This is handy in the desert.

Save the Earth

Ask a grown-up to help you find live lizards to watch. Take along some binoculars to watch them from far enough away so that you won't scare them off. Maybe you'll see them uncurl their long tongues to catch insects.

A Long Time Ago...

As you make the projects in this chapter you can think of the Navajo prayer for inspiration: "May it be beautiful before me. May it be beautiful behind me. May it be beautiful below me. May it be beautiful above me. May it be beautiful all around me."

Fun Fact

One of the important clans of the Hopi people, who live in some of the driest areas, is the Sand-Lizard-Snake Clan.

Did you know that horned toads are actually lizards and that they have a "third eye" in the middle of their forehead? It is really just a photosensitive spot that can sense light and dark, but it does help protect the horned toad from predators.

What You'll Need

- scraps of medium-firm foam. You can get scraps from a foam mattress store. Or use the foam inserts that some electronic items are packaged in.

- For the body you need one piece about 18 to 24 inches long, 3 to 4 inches wide, and 1 to 2 inches thick.

- For the legs you need two pieces about 7 inches long, 1/2 inch wide, and 1/2 inch thick.

- 2 pieces of flexible wire, the thickness of a paper clip but about 6-1/2 inches long. Straightened handles from take-out containers and wires from burned out sparklers work well. You can also buy the wire from a hardware store.

- watercolors, poster paints, or marking pens

- google eyes, or buttons

- a wire coat hanger (or other stiff wire) for the "leash"

- masking tape

- a serrated knife

- scissors

- pliers (to bend wire)

- (optional) a low-temperature glue gun

Caution: Get grown-up help. The glue comes out hot, and the tip of the gun is hot.

- (optional) pinking shears

What to Do

1. Shape the piece for the body with a pointed nose and long pointed tail.

Oops! Don't cut the foam narrower at the neck—it might make the head fall off. You'll form the neck when you squeeze the foam to attach the front legs.

2. Push 1 piece of flexible wire lengthwise into each foam leg piece. Thread it through the center of the entire length. This may be hard to do, but just keep trying. Ask for help if you need it. When the wire is all the way in, use the pliers to bend back any sharp ends of wire sticking out on either end that could cut you.

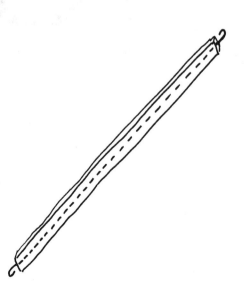

3. To attach the legs, squeeze the body where you want legs, bend the legs in half, squeeze the fold over the top of the body, and twist the wire once around under the belly. Bend the knees and feet to make the legs look realistic. Adjust the shape of the legs so the lizard can stand up.

4. Cut a mouth with the scissors (or pinking shears), and paint or glue on eyes.

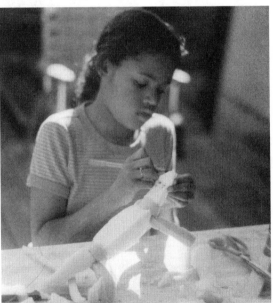

92

5. Decorate the body and legs with paints or pens. Real lizards have stripes, diamonds, and other beautiful patterns. Get a book from the library with photos of lizards to inspire you.

6. Straighten out the hanger. You may need grown-up help, because hanger wire is pretty stiff. Make a 2-inch right-angle bend in one end. Push that end through the neck and into the head. Then you can move the head with the wire and make the lizard look alive. Curve the other end into a handle, and cover over any protruding sharp ends with masking tape.

7. Take your pet out for a walk!

Spun Yarn and Woven Cloth

The first weavers in the Southwest were men. Originally they spun with cotton and used turkey feathers and strips of rabbit skin to make blankets and shawls. In the Pueblo cultures, the men did their spinning and weaving in the kivas. These round, underground rooms served as men's clubhouses and ceremonial rooms and still do today. A kiva has no door in its wall; to get in, the men climb down a long ladder that sticks out of a hole in the ceiling.

When the Navajos arrived in the Southwest, they learned weaving from the Pueblo people, but they made some changes: women did the weaving, and they wove outdoors where there was more light. Later when the Spanish brought sheep, the two native cultures both switched to wool. The Navajos figured out how to dye wool with local plants and began to make intricate patterns with their weaving. At first they made blankets for wearing and ceremonial use, but pretty soon they discovered that visitors (tourists) liked their weaving and would pay good money for it. The Navajos needed money to buy things from the newly arriving traders. Weaving became one of their best ways to make money, and it helped their culture survive and thrive.

Fun Fact

The Navajo language is not similar to other languages in the Southwest. It is most like an Alaskan native language, Athapascan. Navajos use four kinds of tones—low, high, rising, and falling—and it is hard to master them correctly. It is such a difficult language that it is considered impossible to learn as an adult; you have to learn it as a child. It became very useful in World War II as a code language. Navajo men translated battlefield messages into a code based on their language. No one ever broke the code.

Once upon a Time

If you have a younger sibling, read her or him **The Goat in the Rug** by Charles L. Blood and Martin Link, a wonderful story about a Navajo weaver and her goat.

Preparing the Wool

★★

🕐 30 minutes

In this activity, you will clean and untangle the fibers to get them ready for spinning.

What You'll Need

- sheep's wool or goat mohair. You can buy sheep's wool from yarn and craft stores. If you know people who live in a rural place, maybe they can get wool for you from a friend or neighbor.

What to Do

1. Wash the wool or mohair by hand if it's dirty. Ask for grown-up help. Use a small amount of mild soap (not detergent) and lukewarm water. You can soak the wool for a while in the soapy water so that the dirt dissolves out. You want most of the lanolin (natural oil) to stay in the wool. Rinse the wool, spread it in the sun or in a warm room, and let it dry thoroughly.

2. Get the wool ready to spin by pulling it apart by hand (this is called *carding*). Just separate the knotted places, and pull out any sticks or seeds caught in the wool. Pull apart the clumps of wool until it is all fluffed out and there are no more tangles.

Fun Fibers

Yarn can be made from many different kinds of fibers, including rabbit angora, cottonballs, even milkweed fluff. The coast Salish people, from the northwest coast of Canada, used the hair from their small woolly dogs for spinning yarn and weaving. They mixed the dog hair with duck down and fluff from fireweed plants to make blankets and robes. You can try spinning with fun fibers, but wool works the best, since the wool fibers have little scales that catch onto other fibers and hold tight.

A Long Time Ago...

The Alaska Tlingit people spun wild mountain goat hair by hand. Rather than twisting with their fingers, they found it was easier to rub the goat hair on their thighs to twist it. The ancient Hawaiians, who originally came from Polynesia, far away in the Pacific Ocean, used the same method to spin coconut fibers. You can try it too!

Making a Schoolyard Drop Spindle

★

🕐 **15 minutes**

The *whorl* is the weight that helps the stick of a drop spindle keep spinning. The apple here works as a whorl. In Mexico, some spindles are made with a ball of clay around a dowel.

What You'll Need

- a long pencil with an eraser
- an apple with no worms in the core
- a pencil sharpener

What to Do

Sharpen the pencil, and stab it straight through the core of the apple so that about an inch of the point is sticking out.

Using a Drop Spindle

★ ★

🕐 **30 minutes**

When you spin, you twist fibers into a connected, strong, useful material. Yarn can be hand spun by twisting the fibers with your fingers. This is fun and easy, but not very fast. A hand spindle is a simple tool that really speeds up the process. Later, people invented the spinning wheel, which is even faster.

What You'll Need

- 2 feet of strong yarn
- carded (finger-teased) wool
- 1 Schoolyad Drop Spindle

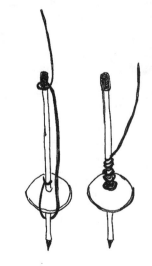

What to Do

1. Tie one end of the strong yarn to the dowel above the apple whorl.

2. Thread the yarn so that it goes around the pointed end of the spindle and up to the eraser as shown in the illustration.

3. Loop the yarn around the eraser and under itself, pulling upward. Cut the piece of yarn so that you have about 3 inches of *leader* (the yarn end to which you connect the wool to spin).

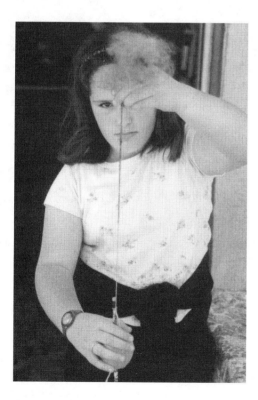

Working Alone

1. Hold the prepared wool and the end of the leader yarn in your *left* hand. Let the spindle hang in the air. With your *right* hand, give the spindle a twist in the clockwise direction.

2. Use your *right* hand to feed the wool slowly down, so that it becomes twisted onto the leader by the spinning spindle. (You make finer yarn by pulling smaller amounts of wool down at a time.) When the spindle slows down, give it another twist clockwise, and continue feeding the wool slowly down so that it gets twisted into yarn.

3. Whether you're spinning alone or in pairs, when the spindle reaches the ground (or you run out of carded wool), unhook the half hitch at the top of the spindle, and wind the new yarn onto the spindle above the whorl. Rehitch the end of the new yarn, leaving three inches of new yarn leader above the eraser at the top of the spindle.

4. Get another bunch of carded wool, and repeat the previous steps.

5. When the spindle is full, wind the yarn into a ball.

6. Use your beautiful yarn to make a headband or a necklace, or weave it on your hanging loom (see the activity that follows).

Yeah! Working in Pairs

1. One person holds the carded wool and the leader yarn, and the other person starts the spindle turning clockwise.

2. The first person slowly feeds small amounts of wool to the leader yarn, creating new yarn, while the second person makes sure the spindle continues to spin evenly.

97

Weaving with a Hanging Loom

★★★

🕐 1-1/2 hours

This loom is a little like a Navajo or Hopi loom, but simpler.

What You'll Need

- wood sticks for the top and bottom of the loom, about 12 inches long and 1/2 to 1 inch in diameter. Driftwood pieces look pretty.

- string, twine, or strong yarn for the *warp* (the lengthwise strings)

- pretty yarn, hand-spun yarn, and strips of cloth for the *weft* (the sideways strings)

- (optional) dried plants that are long, thin, and pretty, such as grasses, flowers, and leaves on stems

- a hand drill or small electric drill

Caution: Get grown-up help with the electric drill. You need to be sure you are using it safely. A small rechargeable drill is the easiest kind to hold.

- a paper clip opened up so that one end can poke string through holes

- scissors

What to Do

1. With grown-up help, drill holes about 1/2 to 1 inch apart in the wood sticks. Hold the wood steady with your foot (not a bare foot!). Drill the same number of holes in both sticks.

2. Cut warp strings about 1 to 2 feet long. Feed each one through a top hole and knot it securely. Then feed each string through a bottom hole in the same order.

Oops! If you have trouble getting the string to go through a hole, push it through with the paper clip.

Yeah! Or just tie the warp threads around the bottom stick.

3. Pull the strings so that they are all the same length and knot them securely on the bottom.

4. Weave the weft yarn over and under the warp threads to form the first row. In the next row, go under where you went over before, and over where you went under, to get a strong fabric. Use your fingers to push the rows of weaving down toward the bottom so you have a solid piece of cloth. If you are making a wall hanging, you can weave in grasses, seed pods, or other beautiful natural materials that are long and thin.

Yeah! If you weave with fat yarn or strips of cloth, the weaving goes much faster.

Oops! Try to make each row the same width. It is easy to pull the weft yarn too hard and have the weaving get narrower and narrower. If that happens, just call it art!

5. You can leave your weaving on the loom and use it as a wall hanging, or cut the warp ends and knot them together in pairs so you have a piece of cloth. You could use it as a Navajo-style rug or Hopi-style shawl for a doll.

Once upon a Time

If you want to know more about Native Americans in the Southwest, read:

The Navajo: Herders, Weavers and Silversmiths by Sonia Bleeker, a good story about a thirteen-year-old Navajo boy.

The Girl Who Chased Away Sorrow: The Diary of Sarah Nita, a Navajo Girl by Ann Turner. This book takes place in 1864, when the Navajos were displaced from their land. Four long years later they were able to return to their land, and since then they have become the largest group of Native Americans.

The Hopis: Pueblo People of the Southwest by Victoria Sherrow has photos, information, and recipes.

Mexican Maracas and Native American Rattles

★

🕐 45 minutes plus 30 minutes

South American maracas were traditionally made of hollow gourds with seeds inside that rattled with a satisfying sound. With one in each hand you could create a complicated dance rhythm. They are now usually made of wood and decorated with carved or painted designs.

Native American rattles are sometimes made of stretched leather with dried seeds inside and are decorated with beads and feathers. They are used in many ceremonies.

We are going to use something surprisingly modern and something gooey to make our maracas or rattles.

Fun Fact

Lightbulbs are made of blown glass by a machine that can blow 2,000 each minute.

What You'll Need

- a burned-out incandescent lightbulb, any size
- plastic wrap or a small plastic bag
- (optional) a wine-bottle cork and tape
- newspaper
- a large bowl
- (optional) a big plastic bag
- 2 cups white flour (whole-wheat flour doesn't work!)
- 2-1/2 cups water
- acrylic paints and brushes or felt-tip pens
- (optional) beads and feathers
- (optional) a low-temperature glue gun

Caution: Get grown-up help. The glue comes out hot, and the tip of the gun is hot.

What to Do

1. Cover the lightbulb with the plastic wrap or small plastic bag to protect yourself from getting cut if the bulb happens to break too early. If your bulb is small, tape a wine cork onto the end of it to make a longer handle.

2. Tear the newspaper into strips. Check the illustration for an easy way to do this.

3. Line the large bowl with the big plastic bag if you want easy cleanup. Mix the flour with the water in the bowl until it feels like cake batter.

4. Dip the strips of newspaper in the flour mixture, and cover the lightbulb with crisscrossing layers of newspaper, until it is covered with 6–8 layers. If any of the layers gets too wet, put on a layer of dry strips to soak up the extra moisture. Cover the entire surface, making sure there are *no* holes. Try to smooth down the last layer so that you can decorate it more easily when it dries.

5. Let the whole thing dry for a day or two. To speed up drying, put it in the sun or use a hair dryer.

6. When it is totally dry, break the glass inside by hitting it with a sharp quick stroke on a hard surface.

Oops! Hit it hard enough to break the glass, but not so hard that you dent the papier-mâché. You will know the glass is broken enough when it rattles nicely.

7. Use the paints or pens to decorate the rattle. Glue on beads and feathers if you want. Then shake it, shake it, shake it.

Calaveras de Azúcar: Sugar Skulls

★★

🕐 1-1/2 hours

Alfeñique (sugar-paste art) is a highly developed skill in Mexico, and it is especially practiced for *El Día de los Muertos*. The Day of the Dead is a time of feasting, dancing, and visiting the graves of loved ones. Many things are made of sugar for kids to enjoy: skeletons, crosses, animals, trees, people, angels, guitars, and baskets of flowers and hearts.

What You'll Need

- 1 cup sugar and 1 teaspoon water for each 3-by-4-inch mold. You need more sugar if your mold is larger.

- a plastic skull-shaped mold. These are sold at hobby shops, cake-decorating stores, or museum shops. Most skull molds have a front and a back, which are made separately and then connected. Very small skull molds are in a single piece.

- icing made of powdered sugar, meringue powder (bought at a grocery or cake-decorating store), and food coloring (ask a grown-up to make it for you, or buy some ready-made icing)

- (optional) small candies for decoration: red hots, small stars, tiny marshmallows, candy confetti, and others from a cake decorating or grocery store

- (optional) shiny metallic paper

- a bowl

- a straight knife or Popsicle stick

- 2 cardboard rectangles slightly bigger than the plastic skull mold

- a cookie sheet

- (optional) a hole punch

A Long Time Ago...

Sugar art is ancient. The Arabs brought the technique to Spain. From there, it came to Mexico and became part of an older indigenous celebration honoring the dead.

El Día de los Muertos

The Day of the Dead is celebrated November 1–2. It is traditional to make **ofrendas** (offerings on an altar) in memory of a dead friend or relative. The **ofrendas** are decorated with beautiful displays of flowers, fruit, sugar skulls, special bread, candles, and things that were special to the dead person. The altars are fun and cheerful, a refreshingly positive way to celebrate life and accept death.

Seems a little scary, but if you are making the sugar skull for an **ofrenda** you put the name of the dead person on the forehead. If you are giving skulls to friends, you write their names on the skulls, and when the friends eat them they are reminded of the sweetness of life.

What to Do

1. Preheat the oven to about 150°F (65°C) with grown-up permission.

2. Mix the sugar and water thoroughly in the bowl. It should feel like damp sand for making sand castles.

3. Pack each half of the skull mold full of the damp sugar. Scrape off the excess sugar with the straight knife or Popsicle stick.

4. Place one cardboard rectangle over the flat sugar side of a half mold, turn the skull over carefully, and put it—cardboard and all—on the cookie sheet. Gently lift off the plastic mold. Repeat for the other half mold.

Oops! If the sugar falls apart as you remove the mold, or the sugar has a crack in it, just dump it back in the bowl and try again.

5. With grown-up help, bake the cookie sheet in the oven for 12–14 minutes until the outside of the skull is hard but the side next to the cardboard is still soft enough to scoop. Check it often to see if it is ready.

Yeah! It will also harden at room temperature but will take at least an hour.

6. Gently scoop out the back of each half of the skull so the skull will be hollow.

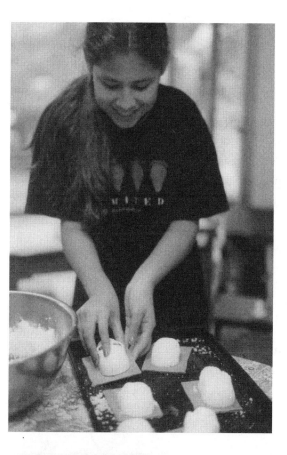

Oops! Don't scoop it so thin that the skull breaks!

7. Glue the front of the skull to the back with the icing.

8. Decorate your skull with the colorful icing and little candies, if you wish. It's traditional to put on shiny eyes made of reflective paper. You can cut circles with a hole punch for eyes and hold them in place with icing.

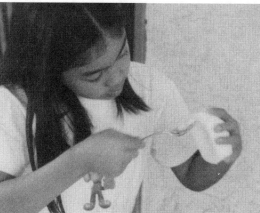

Cowboys

Cowboys are an important part of our American self-image. Their job was to drive herds of ornery cattle from their pastures to the closest railroad, often a thousand miles away. Cowboys had to keep the cattle moving but still let them eat enough to fatten up. At the end, the cattle were shipped east for slaughter. This period in American history only lasted from 1866 to about 1895. We have been given a lot of misinformation about what cowboys were really like. All those TV shows and movies are not accurate (surprise, surprise)!

- Most cowboys spoke Spanish, because many of them were Mexican.

- It wasn't usually "cowboys against Indians." Many cowboys were Native Americans. And other cowboys were friendly with the Native Americans they met on the trail because they wanted to trade with the natives for things they needed.

- About one in four cowboys was African-American. Some came from the South, looking for work. Some slaves in East Texas had learned to ride horses and herd cattle in the 1850s, so they were experienced and ready to work as cowboys for wages when they were freed.

A Long Time Ago...

Cowboy life was very hard and very, very dusty. At the end of the trip, the cowboys just burned their clothes and got new ones!

Juneteenth

The slaves in Texas were not freed until June 19, 1865. To celebrate the freeing of the last slaves in the United States, we now have a holiday called Juneteenth, with parades, barbecues, and fireworks, just like the Fourth of July. Juneteenth is also a time to think about the hard slavery times: to admire the courage of those who survived slavery and those who bravely escaped, and to thank those who helped others escape and those who helped end slavery.

Once upon a Time

Want to read some good stories about cowboys?

The Journal of Joshua Loper, a Black Cowboy by Walter Dean Myers takes place in Texas in 1871.

A Line in the Sand: The Alamo Diary of Lucinda Lawrence by Sherry Garland takes place in Texas in 1836.

Cowboys and Cattle Country by Don Ward looks kind of old-fashioned but has some really good stories of hardship and bravery.

Big Hat

★★

🕐 1-1/2 hours

Most of the inhabitants of the Southwest wore hats—the bigger the better. In Mexico, some people's hats had brims two feet across. Mariachi band players wear hats as big and bright as possible. In the Mexican hat dance, people dance around a ridiculously huge hat. Some ladies in the Southwest used to wear gigantic sombreros with little bells tinkling from the brims. I hope you are inspired to make an even more enormous, silly, fun hat!

What You'll Need

- an old worn bicycle tire. Get one from friends or relatives, or ask at your local bike repair shop. People are usually very happy to have a good use for worn-out tires. You will be using the part called the *bead* by bicycle aficionados (experts), which is a steel wire hoop embedded in the tire next to the sidewalls. Each tire yields two hoops to make two hat rims.

- cloth about 28 inches square or big enough to stretch from rim to rim of the tire with an inch to spare on each side. You can cut old curtains, old sheets, and leftovers from sewing projects to the right size. An old, but pretty, pillowcase will work if you open out the seams. Large old square head scarves and the cloth from broken umbrellas also work!

- a baseball or painter's cap, either new (a cheap one) or used (a cap you don't really want anymore)

- 2 feet of string

- things to decorate your hat with, such as ribbons, lace, rickrack, bias tape, cloth flowers, scraps of cloth, strings of beads, netting, fabric paints, and whatever else you can think of

- a serrated knife

- a low-temperature glue gun

Caution: Get grown-up help. The glue comes out hot, and the tip of the gun is hot.

- scissors

- a pen

What to Do

1. With grown-up help, use the serrated knife to cut through the sidewalls of the tire and remove the two hoops of rubber-encased wire known as the *beads*.

2. Lay out your cloth on a large table or clean floor, pretty side down. Put a wire hoop on top in the center, and glue around under it to attach it to the cloth.

3. Cut around the edge, leaving about 1 to 2 inches for a hem. Fold the hem over the hoop, and glue it down, so that the hoop is no longer visible. Later, you can then cover this hem with decorations if you wish.

4. Measure your head by tying the string loosely around it where you would wear the hat. Then lay the string on the center of the cloth in as perfect a circle as you can. Mark the circle on the cloth.

5. Draw another circle ½ inch inside the first, and cut on the inside circle. This leaves room for a hem.

6. Glue the bill of your baseball or painter's cap to the underside of the hat, and then stretch the rim of the cap around to fit in the circular hole. Pinch together the ½ inch of hem and the elastic rim of the cap so you can glue them all around. You may need help from a grown-up or a talented friend to hold the cap in place as you glue.

Oops! Try not to get low-temperature gun glue on your fingers! If you do, let cool water run on the spot to cool your finger.

7. Now have a wild time decorating your hat. There is no limit to the possibilities. Look at the pictures to see some of the great ideas that kids like you have come up with.

Cork Horse

★★

⏱ 45 minutes

Make a small cork horse and a miniature saddle. For some really cool pictures of horses and saddles, read *Eyewitness Books: Cowboy* by David Murdock and *Man on Horseback* by Glenn Vernam.

What You'll Need

• 7 wine corks

• yarn for the mane and tail

• beads and buttons for the face

• scraps of cloth and leather (real or fake)

• colored pens

• a serrated knife (to cut the corks)

Caution: Serrated knives are pretty sharp. Corks are hard to cut because they are round and small and therefore hard to hold in place. Ask for grown-up help.

• a low-temperature glue gun

Caution: Get grown-up help. The glue comes out hot, and the tip of the gun is hot.

Fun Fact

Miniature horses used to live in North America, but they died out 8,500 years ago. One kind of miniature horse, known as the dawn horse, was the size of a fox, had a body shaped like a rabbit, and had feet more like a dog's! Horses (of a normal size) were reintroduced to America from Spain. They quickly became an important part of the Native American way of life. Apache and Navajo people got horses first. When the Spanish were driven out of New Mexico in 1680, they left behind herds of horses that were traded to groups all over the West. Horses really changed how the Native Americans on the Plains lived. They could hunt buffalo more efficiently, travel faster, and move camp more easily. Later horses were essential for cowboys to do their job.

What to Do

1. Lay out 5 of the corks in the horse shape shown in the illustration, and mark with a pen where to cut 3 of them. Don't worry about the exact angle. Each horse will be unique and adorable. If you don't cut the corks your horse will have stiff legs.

2. With grown-up help, cut the corks on the lines you marked.

3. Glue the pieces together, following the illustration.

4. Glue the last 2 corks onto the feet as "rollers." They will make it possible for the horse to stand up.

5. Use the yarn, beads, and buttons to make the mane, tail, and face.

6. If you like, use pens to color the corks and give your horse unique markings.

7. Use the cloth and leather scraps to make a harness, saddle, saddle blanket, lead rope, straw hat, or other decorations.

Lariat Tricks

Mexican cowboys, called **vaqueros,** were the ones who invented the lariat (a rope lasso for cattle) and many techniques for its use. You can do some pretty neat tricks with a rope, and they are very entertaining to watch. Will Rogers (1870–1935) entertained people with humorous rope tricks. Some of the old tricks are explained in **Cowboy Fun** by Frank Dean.

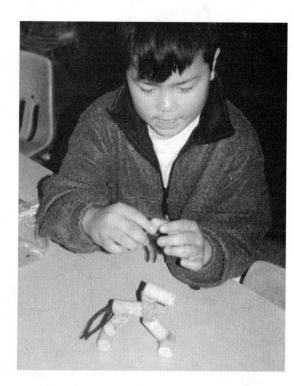

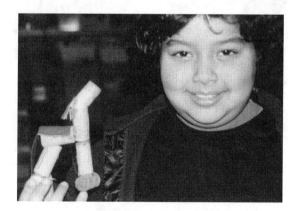

Living on the Edge: The Pacific Rim

L IFE IS MORE VARIED and abundant on the edges of environments than within a single environment. The edge of a meadow has more kinds of plants and animals than the deep forest or the open meadow. The edge of the ocean is richer than the sea or the land. The western coast of the United States, up to Alaska and over the ocean to Hawaii, is all part of the Pacific Rim region. The Pacific Rim is also called the *Ring of Fire* because it is a region of volcanic activity, earthquakes, and upthrusting mountain ranges. Americans come from all over the world, but the Pacific Coast is the place where people from Asia came first and in the greatest numbers. The combination of Native Americans and immigrants from China, Japan, and other countries around the Pacific Rim has created a very rich culture.

Cat's Cradle
★★

🕐 **30 minutes**

String games are found all over the Pacific Rim (and the rest of the world), on islands in the Pacific, in Japan, among the Alaskan native people, and among many other groups of Native Americans (as well as in Africa and South America). Some of the string patterns from these separate corners of the earth are exactly the same! We think of North America as a wonderful experiment in immigration. People have come here from all over the world and created a new culture that is full of ideas from everywhere. But immigration didn't start here. Humans have been migrating all over the globe for about 30,000 years and spreading string games for a lot of that time. It is wonderful to imagine how very, very old this game is. And it's still fun!

What You'll Need

- a string 5–6 feet long knotted tightly to form a circle

- a friend

What to Do

Look at the illustrations to make these shapes:

1. **Cradle.** First person: loop the string around your left palm and around your right palm. Then put your right middle finger under the opposite loop, and pull. Put your left middle finger under the opposite loop, and pull.

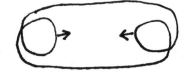

A Long Time Ago...

Some Native American groups in California used the string game to predict or change the weather; some used it to tell whether a baby would be a boy or girl. Some Inuit people play cat's cradle in the fall "to catch the sun in the meshes of the string, and to prevent his disappearance" (**String Figures and How to Make Them** by Caroline Furness Jayne, p. xix). In Hawaii, some string figures have a chant to go with them, and in Alaska some have a song that tells their story. Many cultures have found fun and interest in the complex patterns that can be made with just a string.

112

2. Fish Pond. First person: hold the string in the Cradle position. Second person: pinch the Xs (where the strings cross) with your thumb and forefinger as shown. Then pull out, pull under, and lift up in the center. First person: remove your hands. Second person: open your fingers up and out to get the Fish Pond.

3. Chopsticks. Second person: hold the string in the previous position. First person: pinch the Xs with your thumb and forefinger from the top. Then lift up and out, pull under, and pull up. Second person: remove your hands. First person: open your fingers to get Chopsticks.

4. Manger. First person: hold the previous position. Second person: pick up the string with your right pinkie, and pull it across as shown in the illustration. Then reach through, pick up the other string with your left pinkie, and pull it across. Pinch each thumb and forefinger together, and push them into the triangles shown in illustration. Go in and up. Open your thumbs and forefingers. First person: remove your hands. The Manger is the same general shape as the Cradle, but it is concave (it curves in rather than curving out).

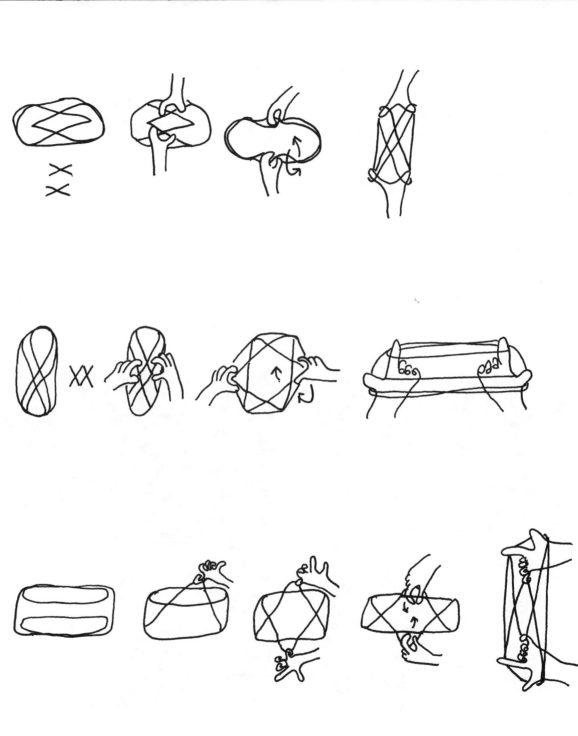

5. Diamonds. Second person: hold the position. First person: pinch from underneath as shown. Bring your hands out, around over the top, and down into the center. Open your fingers out and down. Second person: remove your hands. Diamonds looks like the Fish Pond but is held differently.

6. Cat's Eye. First person: hold. Second person: follow the same process as for the Fish Pond, but since you are starting from a different position, you end up with Cat's Eye.

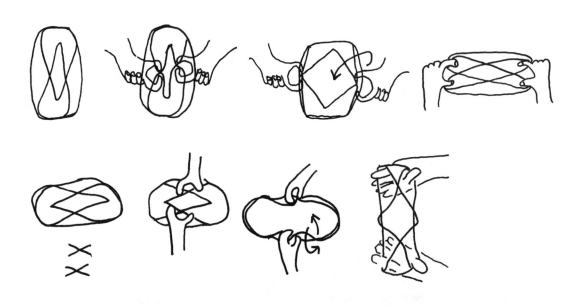

7. **Fish in a Dish.** Second person: hold. First person: pinch with your thumb and forefinger where shown in the illustration. Push in and up. Open out your thumb and forefinger. Second person: remove your hands.

8. **Fish Pond** (again). First person: hold. Second person: pinch the Xs between your thumbs and forefingers, and push down between the two strings in the center of the diamond. Open your fingers to get Fish Pond! First person: remove your hands.

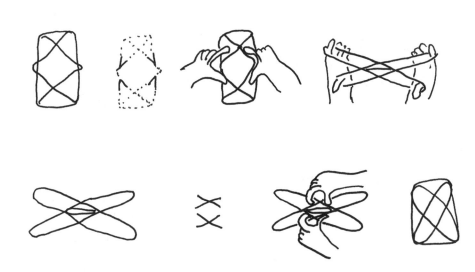

Fun Facts

The string shapes made during the playing of cat's cradle have different names in different countries. The shape we call "Fish Pond" is called "Chess Board" in Korea, "Ghost Cat" in Japan, and "Church Window" in England. I wonder how people came up with these names? The one we call "Cat's Eye" is called "Cow's Eye" in Korea and "Horse's Eye" in Japan. You can probably think of even more original names.

Fun Facts

You can learn more string patterns from one of these two books: **Super String Games** by Camilla Gryski and **String Figures and How to Make Them** by Caroline Furness Jayne. You can also experiment to invent your own. There is an unlimited number of string patterns, so you won't get bored!

Hawaiian Delights

In 1959 Hawaii became our fiftieth state. All the Hawaiian Islands are small, even the eight main ones, and they are way out in the middle of the Pacific Ocean. Almost 2,000 years ago Polynesians managed to discover them, without the help of compass or map. The Polynesian navigation system depended on a person who was highly trained, "the wayfinder," who knew huge amounts of information about stars, birds, waves, winds, currents, islands, and reefs. The trip probably took months. As well as bringing their water and food for the trip, the Polynesians also brought plants they could grow when they arrived: sweet potatoes, gourds, coconuts, bananas, sugarcane, and taro. The starchy taro root is used to make poi, one of their favorite foods.

Fun Fact

Hawaiian hula dance and Alaskan Iñupiaq dance have something in common: they both tell stories with hand movements. Hawaiian hula has a movement vocabulary that tells the old stories and passes on the culture to the young.

High school graduates sometimes are given leis made with dollar bills. A kid might get a lei made of Lifesavers.

Flower Lei

★★

🕐 30 minutes

You can make flower and leaf necklaces, crowns, and hat decorations. If you were going to dance a hula, you would wear them around your wrists and ankles also!

What You'll Need

- a needle: You could use a special lei needle that is about 8 inches long, but a regular needle will do.

- carpet or button thread (or dental floss)

- flowers gathered from a garden or wild area: small roses, pansies, orchids, carnations, bougainvilleas, gardenias, plumerias. Ask for grown-up help to get permission to pick and to identify the plants.

Caution: Do not use oleander flowers. This plant is very poisonous!

- flowers purchased from a wholesale flower market (try *fresh* strawflowers or a "grower's bag" of small carnations)

Oops! Don't buy *dried* strawflowers. They are too tough to get a needle through.

- scissors

What to Do

1. Thread your needle with 4 feet of strong thread, and knot the end.

2. Cut the flower heads off their stems.

3. Organize your flowers in the pattern you want, and string them on one at a time. Push the needle through the center of the stem and out through the center of the flower. For other lei-making techniques, read *Made in Hawai'i* by Jane Fulton Abernethy and Suelyn Ching Tune or *The Hawaiian Lei: A Tradition of Aloha* by Ronn Ronck.

Banana Trick

★★

🕐 30 minutes

Bananas grow well in Hawaii. In fact there were seventy kinds in the old days. Hawaiians used all parts of the plant. Its green leaves made a green dye, and parts of the banana flower made a light-purple dye. Both were used to dye pounded-bark tapa cloth. Dried banana leaves were made into sandals. The fruit was eaten fresh, baked, and dried. Hawaiians from the old times probably didn't try this trick, but they would have enjoyed it! The banana looks normal on the outside but when peeled it is already sliced!

What You'll Need

- a banana
- a needle and a 6-foot piece of thread

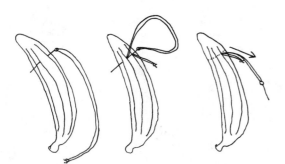

What to Do

1. Thread the needle, and knot the two ends of thread together to make a double thread that is 3 feet long.

2. Stick the needle into the banana skin at a ridge. Make a stitch that goes under the skin but not through the "meat," and bring the needle out at the next ridge. Pull the thread partly through, but leave about 2 inches of thread, with the knot, hanging out.

3. Put the needle back into the exit hole, and go under the skin to the next ridge. Pull the needle out, and repeat until your last stitch comes out where your first stitch started. (Your stitches will circle the banana on the inside.)

4. Thread the needle through the loop of thread near the knot, and pull on the needle. The thread will cut through the "meat" of the banana and exit the first hole, leaving the skin intact.

5. Repeat at different places on the banana to make several cuts.

6. Nonchalantly present the banana to a friend, and convince him or her to peel it right then. Enjoy your friend's look of surprise!

Did You Know?

You may notice that the places where you pierced the banana will start to turn brown. Try soaking the needle and thread in lemon juice before doing this trick. The vitamin C in the lemon stops the browning action of oxygen. Maybe it keeps your body fresh also!

Fun Facts

Take advantage of the browning effect of oxygen to make an "artistic" banana. Make needle marks on a banana skin in pretty patterns. The places you mark will turn brown and will hide the places where you made the stitches for the trick. You could try to convince your friend that you just want to give her or him an artistic banana to eat. Good luck!

Food for Thought

Cut your banana with this trick, but don't peel it until one day later. The sections will be stuck back together! The juices of the banana work like glue.

Chinese Immigration

The story of the Chinese in America is not always a happy tale. Men came originally to make some money and return home to their families. They helped in the California gold rush and in building the western half of the transcontinental railroad. In fact, they became absolutely essential: 9,000 of the 10,000 railroad workers were Chinese. Building the railroad was a competition between those from the East building westward and those in the West building eastward. At first they couldn't get anyone in California to work on the railroad, because everyone wanted to keep looking for gold. When a few Chinese men were hired, the owners discovered that they were good workers and sent off to China to lure more people over. Life was hard in China at that time, so people did want to come to the new country. But building the railroad was very, very hard. It had to be built through the high Sierra Nevada (which means "snowy peaks"). Many people died from the unsafe practices used to blast the tunnels through rock. Even more dangerous was the practice of lowering Chinese workers in baskets over the sides of cliffs to set dynamite into the vertical cliff faces.

Fun Fact

Toilet paper was invented in China in 875! Thank you, thank you!

A Long Time Ago...

Making paper from pulp was invented in China during the Han Empire (202 BCE to 220 CE). The Chinese used mulberry tree bark, hemp, rags, and old fishing nets to make paper! Soon they were making books. Their first dictionary was made in 121 CE. The first English dictionaries weren't written until the 1600s. After the Arabs won a battle with the Chinese in 751, they learned the secret of papermaking from their prisoners. Soon the method reached Europe, and then it leaped across the ocean to America. So, when the Chinese came to California for the gold rush and the railroad, this hugely important invention of theirs had already arrived from the other way around the world!

Deckle and a Mold for Making Paper

★★

🕐 45 minutes

In this activity, you'll make a deckle and mold: the tools you need to make paper.

What You'll Need

- 4 pieces of wood, each 1/2 by 1/2 by 6 inches. Some carpentry shops and lumberyards have a free box where you can get good scraps.

- 4 pieces of wood, each 1/2 by 1/2 by 8 inches.

- a 6- by 8-inch square of fiberglass-mesh window screening. You can cut this from old screens, or buy some screening at a hardware store or home improvement center.

- a staple gun and staples. You can't use a regular stapler because the staples are too small to hold the wood pieces together.

Caution: You will need grown-up help with this tool.

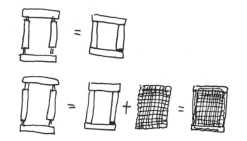

What to Do

1. Make two picture frames 6 by 8 inches. Ask a grown-up to help you use the staple gun to staple the corners securely. Set one of the frames aside to be the deckle.

2. With grown-up help, staple the screening onto the other frame to make the mold.

Pounded Paper

5000 years ago in Egypt a kind of paper called papyrus was made for writing, which is where the word paper comes from. But papyrus is not really paper. Paper is made with a mush and formed on a screen, and papyrus is made of grass stems layered criss-cross and pounded with a hammer. Tapa (made in Hawaii) is also like paper, and 6,000 years old, but it is also not paper. It is pounded bark. Even rice paper (made in Japan) is not paper—and it's not made of rice! It is pounded bark of a special tree. Parchment isn't paper either. It is paper-thin animal skin, in use since about 2,000 years ago.

Saved by the Wasp

Paper is plentiful now, but only 150 years ago it was very precious, because it had to be made out of rags and there weren't enough of them. It took people a while to figure out how paper could be made from trees. In 1719, a French naturalist observed wasps making their nests with digested wood fiber. We think it is obvious now that paper can be made from trees, but it took a creative new way of thinking and a lot of trial and error to make it happen.

Making Paper
★★

⏱ 1 hour

Once you've finished your deckle and mold, you're ready to make as much paper as you want! Each piece of home-made paper will be unique because you get to choose the ingredients.

What You'll Need

- materials for the pulp: plain newsprint, egg cartons, paper bags, used paper, construction paper, colored tissue paper. Torn-up tissue paper works well as a "dye" for your paper.

- materials for texture: dry corn husks, dry flowers, onion skins, straw, thin bark, dry leaves, mulch

- decorations: pressed flowers, flower petals, small fern leaves, tiny feathers, herbs from the kitchen (with permission), sequins, confetti, glitter, bits of yarn

- a blender or food processor

- scissors

- water

- a dishpan (or other pan large enough to hold the deckle and mold)

- a deckle and a mold (see the instructions earlier for making them)

- old sheets or white felt cut into squares about 10 by 10 inches

- (optional) pieces of scrap paper with one side blank

- sponges

What to Do

1. Fill the blender or food processor half full of water. Add some torn up pulp materials. Blend until well mashed, making sure there are no large pieces left. Cut some texture materials and add to the mix. Blend again, but less thoroughly.

2. Pour the mush into the dishpan. If your pan is large, make more than one blender of mush to pour into it. Add water, if needed, to fill the pan about 5 inches deep.

3. With the mold screen side up, place the deckle on top of the mold, and dip them together into the dishpan of mush. Scoop up a nice even layer of pulp. To do this, you need to scoop under enough of the pulp, and then shake the deckle and mold a little as you lift them together.

Oops! If you have the mold and the deckle upside down, you won't be able to get the paper off the screen. If that happens, just shake the mush off of the screen back into the pan, and try again. Everyone does it wrong at least once!

4. Let some water drip back into the pan and then lift off the deckle. This is called the "wet leaf" stage. At this point you can decorate the paper by laying the decorations on top of the wet leaf.

5. Place a square of sheet or felt onto the wet leaf.

6. Turn the mold over, and place it flat on the table. Sponge off any water that seeps through the screen.

7. Gently lift off the mold by starting at one side and peeling it slowly up. Set the mold aside. You can press flower petals and other decorations into the paper at this time also.

8. (optional) Put a square of scrap paper (blank side down) on the top of the homemade paper. Turn the sandwich over and peel off the square of sheet or felt.

9. Lay the homemade paper on a flat place to finish drying (about 24 hours). Put it on an old window screen or cake rack so that the bottom has a chance to dry.

10. You can probably get another, thinner, piece of paper out of the same pulp, or you can blend more pulp to make more paper.

Painted Scroll

★

🕐 **1 hour**

In China and Japan, painting on silk or paper with ink or watercolors is a highly developed art. The pressure and angle of the brush affect the thickness of the lines. The artists believe it is important to use as few brush strokes as possible so that the subject is alive. They study for years to learn to paint with swift and continuous movements. The Chinese and Japanese are masters at birds, animals, and plants. They also enjoy the contrast of scenes that show people in their daily lives in the midst of craggy mountains or large seas. One favorite subject is a solitary person lost in the vastness of nature. For inspiration, see *The Art of China* and *The Art of Japan* both by Shirley Glubok. When Chinese and Japanese people immigrated to the United States, they rolled up their decorative scrolls and brought them along, introducing this art to the Americas.

What You'll Need

- a white or tan pull-down window shade. You can use old ones if they are not torn, or you can buy inexpensive roller shades at a hardware store or home improvement center.

- acrylics paints and permanent marking pens

- newspapers if you'll be painting outside.

- a Styrofoam tray for a paint palette

- a milk carton for the rinsing water

- brushes

- a paint smock (an old shirt worn backward)

124

What to Do

1. Spread out your shade where there is lots of room, on a large table or outside on newspapers spread on the ground. Use a book, rock, or stick to hold the shade open so it won't roll closed while you are painting.

Oops! Make sure you notice which is the top of the shade, so your picture will be right side up.

2. Paint the whole surface.

3. Let the shade dry thoroughly. This may take overnight if the paint is thick.

4. You can mount the shade on brackets at a window or hang it on the wall like a scroll.

Japanese Immigration

Japan is a small country with a large population, so the Japanese are experienced at "intensive agriculture": the know-how to grow lots of food in small spaces and under all sorts of conditions. When they came to Hawaii, California, and Washington, they used these skills to farm land that had been rejected by others as too swampy or too dry, and they made it bloom. They introduced strawberries, blackberries, and raspberries and figured out how to grow celery, which had been a very expensive crop before.

Once upon a Time

If you want to know more about Japanese immigrants, read **Coming to America: Immigrants from the Far East** by Linda Perrin. If you're curious about the Japanese internment in World War II, check out **I Am an American: A True Story of Japanese Internment** by Jerry Stanley and **The Journal of Ben Uchida, Citizen 13559, Mirror Lake Internment Camp, California, 1942** by Barry Denenberg.

A Long Time Ago...

After Japan bombed Pearl Harbor in Hawaii and the United States entered World War II, Japanese-Americans were considered enemies by the American government. President Roosevelt ordered that **all** Japanese-Americans living on the West Coast (Washington, Oregon, California, and Arizona) be evacuated to inland camps. They were given only a few days to get ready to move and most of them lost their homes, businesses, and possessions. The conditions in the camps were very harsh and most of them had to stay there about three years until the war ended. The American government finally apologized to Japanese-Americans in 1988.

Furoshiki: Square Cloth Carryall

★★

🕐 **1 hour**

The cloth carryalls called *furoshiki* (pronounced foo-rosh-key) originated in Japan, and Japanese immigrants brought them to the United States. In Japan, furoshiki are used to carry packages of all sizes. Very large pieces of cloth are used to carry huge bundles on a person's back like an enormous backpack. Small beautiful furoshiki are used to carry gifts, and the cloth is part of the gift. In America, they are used to carry hot dishes to a very American event, the potluck. You can use your cloth to carry a book or a bottle of root beer.

What You'll Need

- a piece of white or light-colored cloth about 1 to 3 feet square (or larger). You can use a white handkerchief or a cloth scrap. Some craft stores carry square cotton "dish towels" that are inexpensive and perfect. If you have an old white sheet, you can cut it into squares and decorate enough furoshikis to give away as presents.

- one or more sets of decorating materials:

- for drawing: permanent pens

- for colored-wax batik painting: wax, crayons, clean tuna cans, a warming tray, cheap paint brushes, an iron, and newspaper

- for tie-dyeing: cloth dyes, water, rubber bands or string, and rubber gloves

What to Do

To decorate your cloth, you can use one, two, or all three of the following techniques.

- **Drawing:** Make wonderful designs with permanent pens. Some traditional furoshikis have intricate plant and bird motifs, and these are easiest to achieve with pens. You can also draw your own family crest (imagined or inherited), either in the center, or around the four corners, so everyone will know that the cloth belongs to you.

- **Batik Painting with Colored Wax:** Melt equal amounts of wax and crayon in a tuna can on a warming tray. Make several colors. Paint them onto the cloth. Then iron the cloth between layers of newspaper to melt the wax out. Pick the iron up and put it down, rather than rubbing it across, so that the wax and color don't smudge too much.

- **Tie-Dyeing:** Use rubber bands or string to bunch the cloth together. Make the bunches tight enough so that the dye won't be able to seep under the tied places. There are really no wrong ways to do tie-dyeing. If you tie the knots tightly you will keep the dye away from more of the cloth. If you tie with string, the lines of white under the string will be more sharply defined. Look at the illustrations to see how these tie-dyed methods work.

- To make a **bull's-eye,** tie a tiny circle, and then tie larger circles around it.

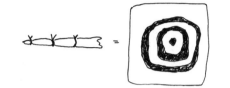

- To make **popcorn circles,** tie a lot of small circles.

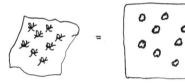

- To make **lines,** fold or roll the cloth, and then tie it with string or rubber bands in several places.

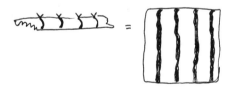

- To make a **spiral,** pinch the center and twist in one direction until it is tight. Hold in place with rubber bands.

1. If you are tie-dyeing, mix the cloth dye according to the directions on the package. Use gloves to protect your hands and dip your tied cloth into the dye.

2. Open it up and let it dry.

Northwest Coast Native Ceremonies

In the bountiful northwestern coastal lands, many Native American groups flourished, each with its special arts and customs. The richness of land made getting food and shelter fairly easy and gave people time to make art. Most impressive were the totem poles and large house fronts carved and painted in wonderful designs. The cedar tree was important to almost every aspect of the northwestern natives' lives. It is one of the most important designs found on their button blanket robes. Whole cedar trees were used for totem poles and to make huge canoes. The natives hollowed out the whole trees for canoes, and then stretched them wider (by softening the wood with boiling water) to make room for more people. Because the land was so full of thick trees, most travel was by sea. Luckily the inland sea was fairly calm and protected.

A Long Time Ago...

In the 1700s and 1800s, Europeans came to the northwest coast for sea otter pelts. The fur trade, which began in 1779, was called the "soft gold rush," because people came and made a fortune from the soft fur. Some of the native peoples became wealthy during the fur trade, but most suffered from this interference in their local culture. The Hudson's Bay Company, which had been active in the fur trade in the eastern U.S. and Canada since 1670, came to the Northwest in the 1800s. They received valuable furs in trade for items useful to the natives, including the wool blankets that were used for dance robes.

Fun Fact

Potlatches are ceremonial feasts where gifts are exchanged in a show of wealth. In preparation for these feasts, robes were decorated with rare shells, feathers, and abalone beads, which were early forms of money. Later money and jewelry were pinned on a blanket and given away. Potlatches are still held for totem pole dedications and other big events.

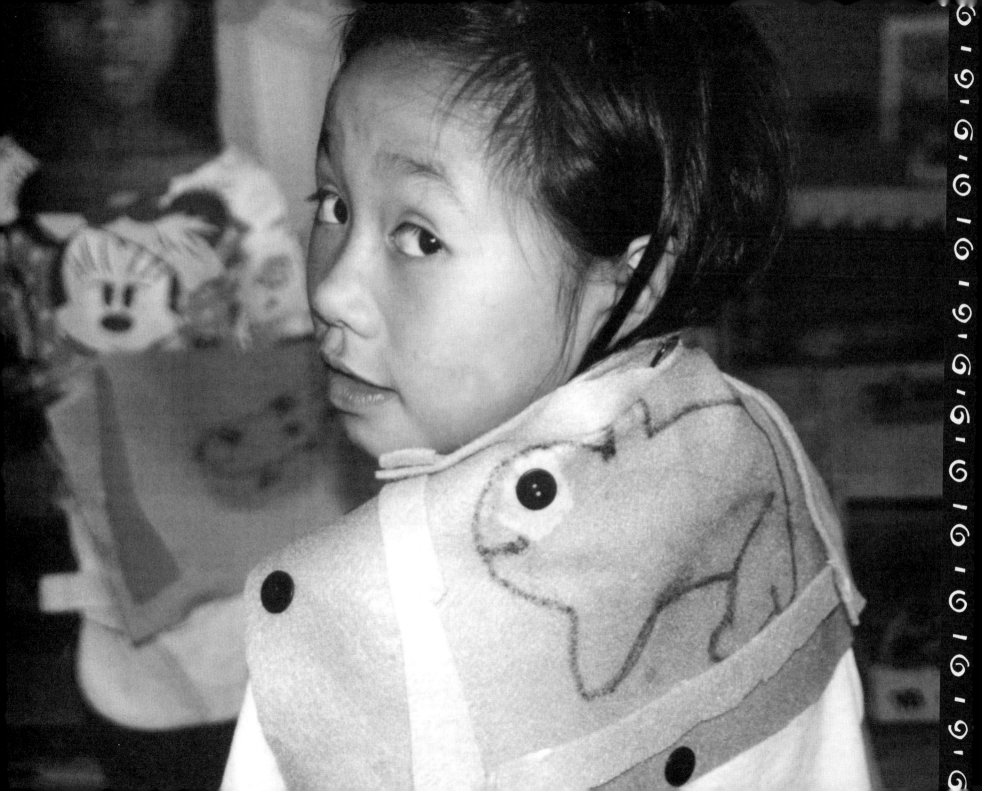

Button Blanket Dance Robe

★★

🕐 1 hour

The northwest coast natives have always made ceremonial robes. At first they used mountain goat wool, cedar bark, or hides. Then, about 200 years ago, Europeans came to their country and brought beautiful buttons from China and strong warm blankets from Europe. The coastal natives found a way to continue their traditions using the new materials. The blankets were turned into ceremonial clothing by using appliquéd red wool and buttons to form crest designs. Traditional blankets were large enough to hang from a person's shoulders down almost to the ground. They were used for dancing. We're going to make a doll-size blanket, but if you want to make a larger one, the process is the same—just use a piece of cloth about 5 to 6 feet by 4 to 4-1/2 feet.

What You'll Need

- felt pieces about 2 by 3 feet (or larger). Red and black or dark blue are traditional colors.

- smallish white buttons or small flat white beads

- a pencil and paper

- a low-temperature glue gun, glue stick, or a needle and thread

Caution: Get grown-up help. The glue comes out hot, and the tip of the gun is hot.

What to Do

1. Plan your design. Traditionally your blanket would show the animal for the clan you were in: eagle, raven, frog, wolf, bear, etc. Think about an animal that you especially like. You might want to choose an animal that has qualities you would like to have. You can leave a space around the top and sides of the blanket for the border of buttons that is traditional.

Oops! No buttons are put on the bottom of the robe. That's so they don't get in the way when you are dancing.

2. Practice drawing a simple line design of your animal on paper. Then pencil it onto the felt.

3. Lay the buttons along the lines of the design and the border so that they almost touch each other in a row. Try to use the same size buttons near each other. When they look right, start gluing or sewing them down. If you are gluing the buttons down, you can use a glue stick although a glue gun works best.

Fun Facts

One of the special foods served at a potlatch was made from the rare soapberry (called **yal is**). A better name is "frothberry." A few tiny berries whip up into a huge amount of white frothy stuff. It tastes really good after you've eaten large amounts of smoked salmon and fish soup!

7

Film and Fantasy: Hollywood

PEOPLE ALL OVER THE WORLD know about Hollywood, the center of American moviemaking. In the early 1900s Hollywood was a quiet place with lots of space and comfortable weather (it never snows and hardly ever rains there). It was a good location for making movies because they could be filmed outside year-round, and it was close to many dramatic landscapes: the Pacific Ocean, the desert, and the rugged mountains.

The first studio to be built in Hollywood was built in 1912, by Sigmund Lupin, whose nickname was "Pop." People loved the short movie he made in 1897 that showed his daughters having a pillow fight. A year later another studio was started in a barn (!) and the actors used the empty horse stalls as dressing rooms. They made Hollywood's first full-length movie in 1914.

In this chapter you can get a chance to entertain your family and friends with your own movie starring *you*.

Find Your Own Stage Name

★

🕐 15 minutes

You need a new exotic name to go with your new exotic identity as a movie star.

What to Do

- Use the name of your first pet as your first name and the name of the first street you lived on as your last name. You're now Gypsy Francisco or Butterscotch Curtis!

- Take all the letters of your name and recombine them into a more glamorous name. You're no longer David Good—you're Vad Dogodi. One British comedy ensemble used only five actors to do Shakespeare's *Twelfth Night,* which has seventeen characters. They managed to pull it off! The playbill credited Paul Gunn's three characters as being played by Alun Pung, Nanu Plug, and Uann Gulp. William Finkenrath's four parts were played by Mathew A. Frillikinn, Matin Fekinwhalli, Wilhelm Ian Inkfart, and Merill Thanifiwank!

Make Shoes with Shazam

★

🕐 30 minutes

If you look the part, you might get the part. Get ready for your acting career by wearing the right shoes!

What You'll Need

- a pair of inexpensive Chinese cloth shoes or an old worn-out pair of your shoes

- strange and beautiful objects for decorations

- paints, pens, and glitter

- a low-temperature glue gun—you really need this tool for this project

Caution: Get grown-up help. The glue comes out hot, and the tip of the gun is hot.

What to Do

Decorate your shoes in any way you want. Look at the photos for a few silly ideas, and then come up with your own. Attach the objects first, and paint second.

Oops! Warm glue will not stick on a wet painted surface.

Put on Makeup

★

⏱ 15 minutes

If you don't have a face-painting kit, ask your mom if she'll let you use some of her makeup.

What You'll Need

- a face-painting kit containing cream or grease makeup

- a paint smock (an old shirt worn backward)

- a mirror

- soap if you use cream makeup; cold cream if you use grease makeup

- facial tissues

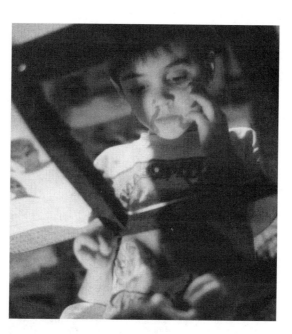

What to Do

1. Don't wash your face first! The natural oils on your skin will protect your face. Put on the smock to protect your clothes.

2. Apply the makeup, smoothing it with your fingers. Grease makeup and cream makeup are both fun to use, but cream cannot be applied over grease. Check out your fantastic face in the mirror.

3. When you want to remove your makeup, wash the cream off with soap and water. To remove the grease, smear on cold cream, and wipe it off with tissues.

A Long Time Ago...

Face paint may have protected the Native Americans from sun, wind, cold, and insects.

137

Create Costumes and Accessories

★

🕐 30 minutes

It is fun to have a huge variety of costumes to choose from. Try to gather lots of stuff for costumes from family and friends.

What You'll Need

Any and all of the following make good costume supplies:

- old Halloween costumes: masks, hats, helmets, capes, furry clothes, doctor's coats, wigs, fake beards, and animal tails

- old junky clothes: men's shirts, fancy dresses, huge pants, black skirts, jackets, stockings or tights

- accessories: clear glasses, dark glasses, belts, canes, purses, gloves, neckties, scarves, jewelry, hats, beautiful shoes, crazy shoes, and pillows to make you appear fat

What to Do

Try some of these ideas:

Squished Face: Change the shape of your face by squishing it with see-through scarves, tights, or stockings.

Animal Ears: Shoulder pads removed from old clothes make instant cute animal ears. Sew them onto a sweatshirt hood or headband or circle of elastic.

Strange Hair

- Unravel old worn-out knitted sweaters and finally have the long curly hair you've always wanted!

- Braid long strands of yarn and have Rapunzel's long hair.

- Glue many braids under the brim of a hat and have dreadlocks.

- Use unwound, unwanted cassette tape for shiny hair. Glue the unruly mass onto a headband or a cap so it will stay on your head.

Plan and Make a Movie

Here's your chance for fifteen minutes of fame! Did you ever want to be sillier, uglier, more smart-alecky, more dorky, more timid, or more brave? In your own movie you can be any character you want. You just need fun friends, a video camera, and some free time.

Once upon a Time

It is complicated to make movies and TV shows. These two books take you through the whole process: **That's a Wrap: How Movies Are Made** by Ned Dowd and **Ramona: Behind the Scenes of a Television Show** by Elaine Scott.

Experiment with the Camera

★ ★ ★

🕐 2–3 hours

What You'll Need

- a blank videotape

- a video camera. If you do not own
  one, borrow one from a friend or relative. You may be able to borrow a
  camera at your local library or school.

- a full-size tripod

What to Do

Earthquake: Shake the camera gently
as the actors react to the "earthquake."

Climbing Walls: Turn the camera
sideways. Find a floor or playground
area that looks like a wall. Make sure
no background is showing (or the
trick will be obvious). The actors lie
on their stomachs and pretend to
struggle up the "wall" (the floor)

Disappearing People: The actors walk
around acting normal, then get a surprised look, and *poof* (you stop

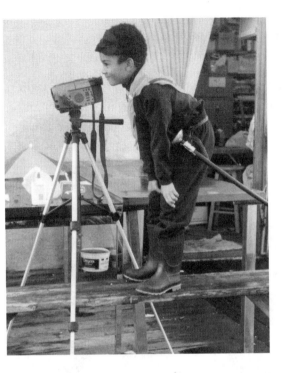

camera, the actors exit, and then you
restart the camera on the empty
space).

Behind a Tree: Find a tree wide
enough for an actor to hide behind.
Record the first actor walking over
and hiding behind the tree. Stop the
camera; the first actor leaves. Then
record the second actor walking over
and going behind tree. Stop the camera again. Repeat as many times as
you wish.

In a Box: Place a large, person-size box
in the camera view. Record one actor
getting into the box. Stop the film
while the actor gets out. Repeat with
lots of actors.

Appearing People: Use the last three
ideas in reverse for another neat
effect.

Find Your Characters

★

🕐 30 minutes

What You'll Need

- a lot of costumes

- (optional, but fun!) a full-length mirror

What to Do

1. Spread out your costumes, and gather your friends.

2. Have all the actors try on different costumes until they find characters they want to be. Give yourselves plenty of time to try on lots of different costumes, until you each find a character that you will enjoy being.

Here are some ideas for Crazy Characters:

- General characters: witches (good and bad), secret agent bus drivers, dead bodies that giggle, butlers, brats, and double-crossing mutts.

- Specific characters: Miss Midnight ("I simply dislike children"), Young Arthur ("I herd the family sheep and keep a rabbit in my room"), Dr. Guin-evere Cyanide ("I'd like to practice on you"), Merkus the Mathemagician ("Where did I leave that formula?").

- One kid I know came up with a story that included Inspector Bob, Woman Vampire, the Vampire's Cat, and the Spy.

A Long Time Ago...

In 1902 the first movie to tell a story was made by a French magician. **A Trip to the Moon** was 11 minutes long, and that was three times longer than the other motion pictures of that time!

Develop the Story

★

🕐 **As long as you want**

1. Decide together how to make a story out of the odd assortment of characters you've picked. Don't make anyone be a character that he or she doesn't want to be; find a way to make a story with everyone being who they want to be. Some people like to develop scenes and material for their story by just fooling around in front of the camera. Other people like to put their ideas down on paper.

2. Spend at least two separate days on the project. On the first day, find your characters and start to plan the story. On the second day, work together to finalize the story and divide it into scenes.

Fun Facts

Half the films made before 1925 were written by women screenwriters. One of them, Anita Loos, was still a schoolgirl when she was paid 15 dollars for her story idea. She continued to write for Hollywood for many years.

Film the Story

★★

🕐 2 hours

What You'll Need

- a video camera and blank videotape
- a full-size tripod
- all your characters in costume

What to Do

- Decide who wants to be the camera operator, or take turns doing it.
- Set up each scene, practice it once, and film it. The simplest method is to do the scenes in order, so that you won't need to do any editing.

Oops! Remind the camera operator to be quiet during filming. Humming and giggling sound very silly on the tape. (I know because I have done both!)

- The person working the camera is responsible for telling the actors when to start and must know when a scene is finished, to stop filming at the right time.
- Keep the story amusing:
- Have a strange character appear in the scene and then realize he is in the wrong movie. For instance: The Big Bad Wolf comes in saying, "I'll huff and I'll puff and I'll . . . oops, wrong movie."
- Have commercial breaks interrupt the story. Most people love to think up hilarious short commercials.
- Have a commentator say, "Pause" (as though pausing the VCR), and have the characters freeze while the commentator comes on screen and makes silly comments about the characters and the plot. Then she says, "Play," and leaves, and the story goes on.

Watch Your Movie

★

🕐 As long as you want

What You'll Need

- a television and VCR
- popcorn

What to Do

- Watch your movie a lot of times! It never gets boring to watch yourself!
- Make a playbill to advertise your movie, and invite your family, friends, and neighbors to come. Make popcorn to share with them.

Make a Fancy Photo Frame for Your Celebrity Self

★

🕐 45 minutes

Now that you are a celebrity, make a really great frame for photos of wonderful, beautiful, famous you!

What You'll Need

- a great, funny, silly, sweet, diabolical, or stupid picture of yourself! Ask your favorite grown-up to take a bunch of pictures of you being you. Or get together with friends and take pictures of each other. Those pictures should be pretty funny!

- anything that looks like a frame: pieces of cardboard, flat boxes, square or heart-shaped candy boxes, shoebox lids, flat Styrofoam or frame-shaped Styrofoam, clear plastic boxes. You just have to look at stuff you would normally throw away and decide if it would make a frame. It is also possible to (gasp) buy a frame!

- decorations: shaped macaroni, glitter, pens, paints, cloth, magazine pictures and words, other collage materials, shells, leaves, cones, other natural materials, ribbons, yarn, aluminum foil, aluminum foil roasting pans, and anything else you can think of

- scissors

- a low-temperature glue gun (with adult supervision only!) or glue stick

Caution: Get grown-up help. The glue comes out hot, and the tip of the gun is hot.

- (optional) a hammer and a blunt nail

What to Do

Almost anything is possible in this project. Here are some ideas:

- Cut out words and other pictures to go with your picture. Paste them on the frame.

- Make a frame, take a photo of you holding the frame, and put the photo of you holding the frame in the frame.

- Make cloth flowers on Styrofoam (the foam needs to be at least 1 inch thick): cut squares or circles of cloth, and use a hammer and a blunt nail to push just the center of the cloth into the Styrofoam. The cloth that sticks out will look like a flower.

- Make a double-photo "book" that opens, or a triptych (a set of three pictures). Make a photo cube with four photos around a box or clear plastic packaging cube.

- Cut your photos and reconnect them in funny ways.

- Cut aluminum foil roasting pans into suns, moons, and animal shapes to decorate the frame.

- Make a rustic frame with natural materials and macaroni shapes.

- Make a valentine photo to give as a present, by using a heart-shaped candy box or by gluing hearts onto the frames.

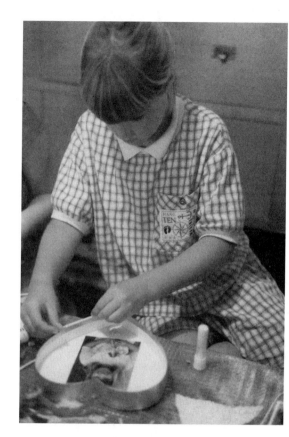

BIBLIOGRAPHY

Tea Taxes and Eye Patches: Colonial America

Arden, William. *Alfred Hitchcock and the Three Investigators in the Mystery of the Dead Man's Riddle.* (Based on characters created by Robert Arthur.) New York: Random House,1974.

Dana, Richard Henry. *Two Years before the Mast.* Cleveland and New York: World Publishing Co., 1946.

Denenberg, Barry. *The Journal of William Thomas Emerson: A Revolutionary War Patriot.* My Name Is America Series. New York: Scholastic, 1998.

Earle, Alice Morse. *Home Life in Colonial Days.* New York: Macmillan Co., 1899.

Gardner, Martin. *Codes, Ciphers and Secret Writing.* New York: Dover, 1972, 1984.

Gould, Roberta. *Making Cool Crafts and Awesome Art.* Charlotte, VT: Williamson, 1998.

Gregory, Kristiana. *The Winter of Red Snow: The Revolutionary War Diary of Abigail Jane Stewart.* Dear America Series. New York: Scholastic, 1996.

Jansson, Tove. *The Exploits of Moominpappa.* New York: Farrar, Straus & Giroux, 1994.

Lasky, Kathryn. *A Journey to the New World: The Diary of Remember Patience Whipple.* Dear America Series. New York: Scholastic, 1996.

Melville, Herman. *Moby Dick.* Berkeley: University of California Press, 1979.

Osborne, Mary Pope. *Standing in the Light: The Captive Diary of Catharine Carey Logan.* Dear America Series. New York: Scholastic, 1998.

Poe, Edgar Allan. "The Gold Bug." In *Complete Stories and Poems of Edgar Allan Poe.* Garden City, NY: Doubleday, 1966.

Stevenson, Robert Louis. *Kidnapped.* New York: Dodd, Mead, 1949.

Stevenson, Robert Louis. *Treasure Island.* New York: Scribner, 1981.

Tolkien, J. R. R. *The Hobbit.* Boston: Houghton Mifflin, 1978.

Twain, Mark. *The Adventures of Tom Sawyer.* New York: J. Messner, 1982.

Wilder, Laura Ingalls. *The Little House in the Big Woods.* New York: Harper & Row, 1953.

Eat, Drink, and Be Merry: North Country Pioneer Life

Earle, Alice Morse. *Customs and Fashions in Old New England.* New York: Charles Scribner's Sons, 1893; reprint, Detroit: Singing Tree Press, 1968.

Earle, Alice Morse. *Home Life in Colonial Days.* New York: Macmillan, 1899.

Hamerstrom, Frances. *Walk When the Moon Is Full.* Trumansburg, NY: Crossing Press, 1975.

Wilder, Laura Ingalls. *Farmer Boy.* New York: Harper & Row, 1953.

Wilder, Laura Ingalls. *The Little House in the Big Woods.* New York: Harper & Row, 1953.

Wilder, Laura Ingalls. *On the Banks of Plum Creek.* New York: Harper & Row, 1953.

Hain't Much, but You're Welcome to It: Southern Country Roots

Chase, Richard. *Grandfather Tales.* Boston: Houghton Mifflin, 1948.

Chase, Richard. *The Jack Tales.* Boston: Houghton Mifflin, 1943.

Courlander, Harold. *Terrapin's Pot of Sense.* New York: Holt, Rinehart & Winston, 1957.

Funk, Charles Earle. *Thereby Hangs a Tale: Stories of Curious Word Origins.* New York: Harper & Row, 1950.

Gorrell, Gena. *North Star to Freedom: The Story of the Underground Railroad.* New York: Delacorte Press, 1996.

Hamilton, Virginia. *The People Could Fly: American Black Folktales.* New York: Alfred A. Knopf, 1985.

Hoyt-Goldsmith, Diana. *Cherokee Summer.* New York: Holiday House, 1993.

Hudson, Wade, and Cheryl Hudson. *How Sweet the Sound: African-American Songs for Children.* New York: Scholastic, 1995.

McKissack, Patricia C. *A Picture of Freedom: The Diary of Clotee, a Slave Girl.* Dear America Series. New York: Scholastic, 1997.

Payton, Sheila. *Culture of America: African Americans.* New York: Marshall Cavendish Corp., 1995.

Ross, Gayle. *How Rabbit Tricked Otter and Other Cherokee Trickster Stories.* New York: HarperCollins Publishers, 1994.

Tunis, Edwin. *Indians: Revised Edition.* New York: Thomas Y. Crowell, 1959.

Westridge Young Writers Workshop. *Kids Explore America's African-American Heritage*. Santa Fe, NM: John Muir Publications, 1992.

Tenderfeet and Greenhorns: The California Gold Rush

Andrist, Ralph, and the Editors of American Heritage. *The California Gold Rush*. New York: American Heritage Publishing Co., 1961.

Bloch, Louis M., Jr., ed. *Overland to California in 1859: A Guide for Wagon Train Travelers*. Cleveland, OH: Bloch and Co., 1984.

Blumberg, Rhoda. *The Great American Gold Rush*. New York: Bradbury Press, 1989. Quoting J. S. Holiday, *The World Rushed In: The California Gold Rush Experience* (New York: Simon & Schuster, 1981).

Calhoun, Mary. *Medicine Show: Conning People and Making Them Like It*. New York: Harper & Row, 1976.

Firnstahl, Timothy. *Jake O'Shaughnessey's Sourdough Book*. San Francisco: San Francisco Book Co., 1976.

Groh, George W. *Gold Fever: Being a True Account, Both Horrifying and Hilarious, of the Art of Healing (So-Called) during the California Gold Rush*. New York: William Morrow & Co., 1966.

Oakland Museum of California. *Gold Fever: The Lure and Legacy of the California Gold Rush*. Museum exhibit, Oakland, CA, 1998.

Reader's Digest. *America's Fascinating Indian Heritage*. Pleasantville, NY: Reader's Digest Association, 1978.

Lizards and Skulls: The American Southwest

Bleeker, Sonia. *The Navajo: Herders, Weavers and Silversmiths*. New York: William Morrow & Co., 1958.

Blood, Charles L., and Martin Link. *The Goat in the Rug*. New York: Four Winds Press, 1976.

Carmichael, Elizabeth, and Chloë Sayer. *The Skeleton at the Feast: The Day of the Dead in Mexico*. Austin: University of Texas Press, 1992; London: British Museum Press, 1991.

Dean, Frank. *Cowboy Fun*. New York: Sterling Publishing Co., 1980.

Garland, Sherry. *A Line in the Sand: The Alamo Diary of Lucinda Lawrence*. Dear America Series. New York: Scholastic, 1998.

Harris, Zoe, and Suzanne Williams. *Piñatas and Smiling Skeletons: Celebrating Mexican Festivals*. Berkeley, CA: Pacific View Press, 1998.

Lasky, Kathryn. *Days of the Dead*. New York: Hyperion Books for Children, 1994.

Murdock, David H. *Cowboy*. Eyewitness Books. New York: Alfred A. Knopf, 1993.

Myers, Walter Dean. *The Journal of Joshua Loper, a Black Cowboy*. My Name is America Series. New York: Scholastic, 1999.

Schlissel, Lillian. *Black Frontiers: A History of African American Heroes in the Old West*. New York: Simon & Schuster Books for Young Readers, 1995.

Sherrow, Victoria. *The Hopis: Pueblo People of the Southwest*. Brookfield, CT: Millbrook Press, 1993.

Trimble, Stephen. *The Village of Blue Stone*. New York: Macmillan Publishing, 1990.

Turner, Ann. *The Girl Who Chased Away Sorrow: The Diary of Sarah Nita, a Navajo Girl*. Dear America Series. New York: Scholastic, 1999.

Vernam, Glenn R. *Man on Horseback*. New York: Harper & Row, 1964.

Ward, Don. *Cowboys and Cattle Country*. New York: American Heritage Publishing Co., 1961.

Living on the Edge: The Pacific Rim

Abernethy, Jane Fulton, and Suelyn Ching Tune. *Made in Hawai'i*. Honolulu: University of Hawaii Press, 1983.

Denenberg, Barry. *The Journal of Ben Uchida: Citizen 13559, Mirror Lake Internment Camp, California, 1942*. My Name Is America Series. New York: Scholastic, 1999.

Glubok, Shirley. *The Art of China*. New York: Macmillan Co., 1973.

Glubok, Shirley. *The Art of Japan*. New York: Macmillan Co., 1970.

Gryski, Camilla. *Super String Games*. New York: Morrow Junior Books, 1987.

Jayne, Caroline Furness. *String Figures and How to Make Them: A Study of Cat's-Cradle in Many Lands*. New York: Dover Publications, 1962.

Jensen, Doreen, and Polly Sargent. *Robes of Power: Totem Poles on Cloth*. Vancouver: University of British Columbia Press, 1993.

Okudaira, Hideo. *Narrative Picture Scrolls*. New York: Weatherhill; Tokyo: Shibundo, 1973.

People of 'Ksan. *Gathering What the Great Nature Provided*. Seattle: University of Washington Press, 1980.

Perrin, Linda. *Coming to America: Immigrants from the Far East*. New York: Delacorte Press, 1980.

Ronck, Ronn. *The Hawaiian Lei: A Tradition of Aloha*. Honolulu: Mutual Publishing. 1997.

Stanley, Jerry. *I Am an American: A True Story of Japanese Internment*. New York: Crown Publishers, 1994.

Film and Fantasy: Hollywood

Dowd, Ned. *That's a Wrap: How Movies Are Made*. New York: Simon & Schuster Books for Young Readers, 1991.

Scott, Elaine. *Ramona: Behind the Scenes of a Television Show*. New York: Morrow Junior Books, 1988.

INDEX

About the Author

Roberta Louise Gould has a B.A. in biology from Antioch College, Yellow Springs, Ohio (1969), an M.A. in psychology from California State University, Sonoma (1976), and many years' experience teaching creative arts. She ran a children's cultural education program at the Alaska State Museum in Juneau and has worked with kids in New Hampshire, New York, Michigan, Kentucky, and California. Since 1990 she has organized and run an after-school arts and summer adventure program called "Bobbie's Amusing Muses" in Albany, California. She has done volunteer art enrichment in a Richmond, California, elementary school since 1996.

Bobbie has had many experiences that led to the creative projects in this book:

- **Tea Taxes and Eye Patches:** When she was thirteen, she took sailing lessons on a little lake. She wondered why the instructor always paired her up with a boy in the small boats. At the end of the week the instructor finally noticed that she was the person whose nickname was Bobbie, and she was obviously not a boy!

- **Eat, Drink, and Be Merry:** She taught at a farm school in Upstate New York and went on a lot of snowshoeing trips with children. They all laughed when they kept falling off the compacted snow trail and landing head down in the deep soft snow. Have you ever tried to get up out of soft snow with great big (old-fashioned) snowshoes on your feet?

- **Hain't Much, but You're Welcome to It:** Bobbie lived on a holler in Kentucky with a family that had sixteen children and only four beds. She slept with the little girls—three beside her and one across the bottom of the big old feather bed.

- **Tenderfeet and Greenhorns:** She was born in California and her children were born in California. But her first 'kid' was Mindy-Goat, who lived in the backyard and always tried to rush indoors when the door was opened.

- **Lizards and Skulls:** The author, her husband, and her three sons attended a Navajo dance contest at which they were almost the only non-native people. Part of the event was a raffle to raise money for the local school. It was a lottery, so Bobbie's lucky middle child chose the number, and of course he won. The family was embarrassed to leave carrying the grand prize, a huge cake covered with tons of icing.

- **Living on the Edge:** In Juneau, Alaska, Bobbie lived in a cabin that was 10 by 20 feet. She once bicycled over to a friend's house, leaned her bicycle against the back of his car, borrowed the keys to the car, and then, without thinking, backed up over her own bicycle, crunching her main form of transportation.

- **Film and Fantasy:** She has no story of movie stardom—yet!

152